MW01122913

Last

Job Search

Tips

By
Brandon Toropov

CAREER PRESS
3 Tice Road
P.O. Box 687
Franklin Lakes, NJ 07417
1-800-CAREER-1
201-848-0310 (NJ and outside U.S.)
FAX: 201-848-1727

LAST MINUTE JOB SEARCH TIPS
İSBN 1-56414-239-6, $7.99
Cover design by Foster & Foster
Printed in the U.S.A. by Book-mart Press

To order this title by mail, please include price as noted above, $2.50 handling per order, and $1.00 for each book ordered. Send to: Career Press, Inc., 3 Tice Road, P.O. Box 687, Franklin Lakes, NJ 07417.

Or call toll-free 1-800-CAREER-1 (NJ and Canada: 201-848-0310) to order using VISA or MasterCard, or for further information on books from Career Press.

Library of Congress Cataloging-in-Publication Data

Toropov, Brandon.
    Last minute job search tips / by Brandon Toropov.
        p. cm.
    Includes index.
    ISBN 1-56414-239-6 (pbk.)
    1. Job hunting--United States.   I. Title.
    HF5382.75.U6T673   1996
    650.14--dc20   96-4049
                                                                    CIP

To
David, Stephen and Julia

Acknowledgments

Ron Fry's vision, patience and guidance helped to bring this book into existence; other people who played an invaluable role in helping me with this project include Glenn KnicKrehm, Leslie Tragert, Bob Tragert, Henry Tragert, Mary Tragert and, last but not least, my wife Mary Toropov, whose ability to put up with the various inconveniences of being married to a writer never ceases to amaze me.

Contents

Introduction

You need a job. Fast.

This book will offer you a detailed program that will help you track down the job you deserve—in short order. The timelines it presents are *rough* approximations of how long it should take to see the results you're after if you incorporate the ideas laid out in each chapter. Obviously, no two cases are alike, and no two employment situations will require exactly the same steps. All the same, it is my conviction that if you follow the advice that follows in a conscientious, upbeat fashion, you *will* get the right job—and without having to wait for months on end.

If I had to boil this book down into a single sentence, it would read as follows:

People like to hire those who show persistent optimism.

The varying forms that persistent optimism can take, and some specific suggestions on using it to generate results for you on the job front, are the subject of what follows.

It's normal at this point of the book to wish the reader "good luck." I'm not going to do that, because you don't need luck. In fact, luck doesn't even exist. All that exists is preparation, attitude and the willingness to develop and act upon opportunity. As you set out to use the system this book presents, I wish you all you really need for success on the job front and in the business world: the right outlook, and a willingness to keep coming back to the game plan.

—B.T.

Chapter 1

You

A few preliminaries

In the middle of difficulty lies opportunity.
—Albert Einstein

Much of the advice that follows in this book will appeal to your ability to contact prospective employers directly—either on the phone or in person—and make a positive impression *very, very quickly.*

The best way to do this is to relay *success stories* that illustrate some positive aspect of your career, and to do this in an upbeat, optimistic manner.

Although the facts you present matter a great deal, the *way* you pass along your success story will probably be more important initially to the prospective employer than the particulars of the story. When you contact someone directly to make your case for employment, you are *demonstrating how you are likely to react to stressful or demanding situations.* Keeping your cool and delivering the good news in a poised, confident, upbeat way is the best strategy you can follow for getting a job offer quickly.

In this first chapter of the book, you'll find some essential advice on developing and delivering the success stories that will help you get a job quickly. We'll also talk a little bit about phone technique. *Don't skip this part of the book!* The rest of the chapters won't make much sense without it.

The success of most things depends upon knowing how long it will take to succeed.
—Baron de Montesquieu

Research

You may have a little research to conduct before you can put the ideas in this book to best use. The advice that follows assumes that you have some basic idea of the ways of doing business in the industry you want to work in, and that you know—roughly—the type of work you want to do in that industry. If you don't know much about either of these points, you should head to the library and sort out your priorities, because *a firm sense of purpose* may be your most valuable asset when dealing with prospective employers.

Your goal should certainly be broad enough to incorporate the various opportunities you're likely to come across, but it should nevertheless be a clear goal, one you can articulate in a single sentence. You will get much better results by saying, "My aim is to be a technical writing specialist at a Fortune 100 company in the New York City metropolitan area," than you will by saying, "I can do anything."

Your list of target employers

If you have not already done so, you should use the resources of your local library to develop a target employer list, and to acquaint yourself with the current trends in your target industry and the duties of the job you have in mind.

You can develop your list of target employers from a variety of sources, including:

- Industry trade magazines.
- Local and national business directories.
- National business publications such as *The Wall Street Journal* or *Business Week*.
- Your local newspaper.
- Local employment directories that feature listings of employers.

In addition, you should also use the library to find out as much as you can about any specific company from which you hope to win a job. If the library's resources—including magazine articles, annual reports and online information services—do not provide you with at least five to 10 pages of solid factual material about a company you are targeting, call the organization yourself and ask for sales catalogs, employee information packets or other resources. (Intrepid job seekers have been known to buy a single share of stock in the target company so as to get the best and latest information on the company.)

---

*If the single man plants himself indomitably
on his instincts, and there abide, the huge world
will come round to him.*

—Ralph Waldo Emerson

Find the *right* job

Let's say you're unsure about the industry you want to enter, the kind of organization you hope to work for or the kind of job you want to hold. You should probably meet with a career counselor at your school or *alma mater* and ask for some help in focusing your search. Getting the job *fast* is only part of the equation...although when you're worrying about finding the money to pay the rent, it's certainly an important part. But landing in the *right* job counts for something, too.

Fortunately, you're likely to find a job in short order if the employment area you're pursuing is one that reflects a genuine, deeply felt passion on your part. Employers can tell when you're in the game for the love *and* the money, and they know that people who fit this description generally make the best (and happiest) employees.

That said, the sad fact remains that in the world of work we live in today, employers don't give guarantees. Margins are tight; competition, both foreign and domestic, is brutal; technology is advancing at a dizzying pace. If it will help a company's margin to let an employee go who seems a little less self-directed, a little less amenable to change, a little more likely to throw up his or her hands when things go wrong, then guess what? The company will find a way to let that employee go. (And sometimes, of course, today's organizations engage in wholesale "body reduction" campaigns that have little—or nothing—to do

---

with one's attitude or job performance.) This is a fact of working life at the dawn of the 21st century: In order to become as efficient as the competition, or take advantage of a new advance in design or computerization, *the company will let you go.*

To many, this dynamic, low-commitment way of dealing with workers appears heartless, because it is so much less predictable than the employment environment of a decade or more ago. All the same, this environment is what we have to work with.

Yet the news is not all bleak. If we can *adapt* to the sudden-shift, bottom-line-first mindset today's employers have assumed, we can actually make the rules of the game work in our favor. And wouldn't *that* be nice for a change?

About one-fifth of the people are against everything all the time.
—Robert F. Kennedy

The demeanor you present in your direct contacts with potential employers, as much as any of the formal experiences you have had in the workplace, will serve instant notice that you represent the kind of employee businesses need—today.

That's right. The *how* of what you say to employers, as well as the *what,* must address three of the most important concerns of today's decision-makers. In just a moment,

you're going to begin the process that will help you demonstrate to employers that you can address those concerns.

---

*The man who makes no mistakes does not
usually make anything.*
—Bishop W.C. Magee

Three messages

You probably already know this, but it's worth noting
that ours is a time of great change. Lifelong careers with
one benevolent employer have pretty much gone the way
of the buggy-whip. Why? Well, for one thing, *today's companies have to react more quickly and effectively than ever
before* to the challenges they face in the marketplace. As
crazy as the *employment* world may look to you, you may
rest assured that the world of *marketing and entrepreneur-
ship* looks even more unpredictable to the people who are
trying to build profitable companies. We live in a world in
which "international companies" can be formed—and can
be successful—more or less overnight, thanks to a snazzy
home page on the World Wide Web. We live in a world in
which demand for once-essential products and services can
be superseded in an instant as a result of new technologi-
cal developments.

For the prospective employer, and for you, *adaptability
is everything.*

In today's economy, a work force made up of people
who can each perform a single set of tasks quite well can
actually be a serious handicap to the company you're trying to work for. If each worker's focus is on a narrowly
written job description, rather than addressing new business

---

problems with creative solutions that may reach into previously uncharted areas, the company may not be able to react effectively to competitive challenges or market shifts.

This means you have to forget all about conventional job descriptions. Your last one, your present one, the one you think may be attached to your job, the one that shows up in the paper this morning. *All of them.* Instead, you must find—and memorize—success stories from your personal history that show your willingness, ability, and, yes, your *eagerness* to work outside that job description.

"It's not my job" is an obscenity on the employment front these days, so don't say it. As a general rule, today's employers are on the lookout for workers who show the ability to adapt well to *brand-new* ideas and procedures. They *want* to talk to people who can show a little initiative when circumstances dictate—which is most of the time. By passing along stories that demonstrate that you are this kind of person, you will make them want to hear more from you.

Message number 1: *When you use the ideas in this book, you must incorporate success stories that demonstrate your ability to* **adapt well to new ideas and procedures,** *and show that you are not wedded to the narrow confines of a written job description.*

This does not mean you should tell the employer you can "do anything"! It means you should demonstrate a specific set of skills in a certain area...and a willingness to adapt those skills to *other, unexpected problems* as they arise.

To get the most from this book, you must prepare *compelling success stories* that highlight this trait. Start working on them right now. On a sheet of paper, take a few moments now to jot down the details of five separate occasions in your work, educational or volunteer history when you adapted well to a new setting. You can probably come up with a lot more than five examples!

It's not really that difficult. Think of the times you pitched in when a supervisor was ill, or mastered a new piece of computer software in short order, or performed well when given a new set of responsibilities in an area where you had little or no experience. Take the time *right now* to specify some details of *at least* five such experiences. Use nonwork-related examples if, after 10 or 15 minutes, you are still having trouble identifying such stories from your work history. Here are some examples of what your stories might sound like. Be sure, though, to incorporate *your own* experiences, not to simply adapt what follows to your own situation. Don't exaggerate; *do* make the most of the positive, can-do adaptability stories in your own background.

All things are ready if our minds be so.
—William Shakespeare

Success stories: adapting to new situations

"We were launching a new product, and the director of marketing wanted to ship out some free samples to a number of important retailers. There were about 2,000 samples. The problem was that this person's

*assistant, who would normally have handled the
data entry portion of the job, was out with the flu
that week, and the samples had to arrive before a
major national television promotion that couldn't be
rescheduled. I volunteered to stay late three nights
that week and do the entry work on the director of
marketing's computer system—even though I was
technically part of the accounting department. Well,
it worked out quite well—the mailing of free samples
went out right on time, and the director of
marketing made a point of submitting a written
thank-you note for inclusion in my salary review
that year. I think that might have had something to
do with the nice raise I got, to tell you the truth."*

හ හ හ හ හ

*"At my last job, I really wanted to work in the
publicity department after having spent six months
in shipping. I talked to the woman who did the
hiring and asked her what I had to do to be
considered for the job. She told me she was
concerned about my telephone skills. So I did some
work at home with a tape recorder and listened to
my own vocal delivery, and I practiced for a week or
two. After I heard an improvement, I took the tapes
to the woman in publicity and asked her what she
thought. She put the transfer through that week."*

හ හ හ හ හ

*"One week, the operations manager was sick and I
was put in charge of the department by default.*

17

There was an unexpected delivery from a shipper that no one had told me about. I learned later that it was about two weeks early. At the time, I really wasn't sure what I was supposed to do, and I couldn't reach anyone on the phone. There was absolutely no room in the warehouse to store the shipment. But I knew the merchandise that was coming in was something the president of the company had been talking about at a big meeting with my boss, so I authorized a temporary rental of some warehouse space. That way, we didn't have to refuse the shipment and send it back to the manufacturer. It was a lucky thing I did—the manufacturer was located in Seoul, Korea!"

Profit orientation and efficiency

The second major piece of information you need to pass along to the employer has to do with *profit orientation and efficiency*. In the current employment world, those who live simply to "punch the clock" are the first to be let go. If you want to win the job offer you truly deserve, you'll have to find a way to convey, in a compelling way, your desire to accomplish a little bit more than sit quietly, fill out expense reports once a month, and submit your picks to the office football pool. Prospective employers *want* to talk to people who won't require any convincing that the reason people show up for work in the first place is to help the organization attain its primary goals—in the private sector, that means making money. (In the public or nonprofit sector, you need to demonstrate your ability to help the organization operate at prime efficiency.)

> Message number 2: *When you use the ideas in this book, you must incorporate success stories that demonstrate your ability to **help the organization operate efficiently**, and that you are determined to deliver the profits and/or results the prospective employer must commit to.*

You must therefore prepare several *quantifiable* examples of your on-the-job ideas, or of the problems you've resolved (or helped to resolve) in the workplace. What have you done that has led to savings or increased revenue for the organization you worked for? Use specific figures to cite improved performance in a particular area. Did you supervise a sales staff that posted a *170-percent increase over the year?* Did you help to bring a product to market *eight weeks ahead of schedule?* Did a new idea you suggested result in *six fewer absences every year per employee?*

Take some time now—at least 20 to 30 minutes, and perhaps as much as 90 minutes—to develop as many examples of your efficiency and profit orientation as possible. You'll strengthen your case if you can appeal to independent sources: quotes from your own salary reviews, annual company reports, sales reports, commission checks and so on. Make every effort to use *actual figures* to bolster your success stories. If you must give estimates, be sure they're responsible, and note that they are estimates.

The process may be difficult at first, but stay with it. How much would it cost your employer if you simply refused, for a whole day, to do any of the things you normally do on the job? What was the last crisis or emergency situation that you helped to resolve? What would have happened if you had done nothing?

Don't cheat yourself. Take the time now to develop this list of events. Doing so will be one of the most important tasks of the entire preparation phase of your job search campaign. These stories are perhaps the most important features of your job search campaign; most of the ideas that follow in this book will be useless if you cannot quantify the solutions you've delivered in the past for other employers.

Success stories: efficiency and profit orientation

"On my January performance review, I was cited as, quoting here, 'a positive, upbeat force who's a real plus for the entire department.' My supervisor recommended a 14-percent raise, the highest he was allowed to submit. I think the main reason for that choice was my work on the 'Vocabulab' project, which I more or less developed from scratch, and which sold 35,000 units during its first year of release."

෨ ෨ ෨ ෨ ෨

"My overtime work on the Peterson project allowed us to submit our bid two days earlier than we would otherwise have done. If I hadn't put that time in, I honestly believe we would have missed the deadline—and lost a $200,000 project."

෨ ෨ ෨ ෨ ෨

"By setting up a car pool and phone tree in my department, I was able to reduce weather-related absenteeism by 25 percent, compared to the same period of the previous year. My boss told me that he thought I'd saved the company at least two person-weeks in lost productivity over the course of the year."

The last message you'll be getting across to employers can be best described as *market orientation*. This means knowing what makes for a good sales presentation, and being willing to give one when the situation demands, whether your job description has anything to do with sales or marketing. You must show that you have a sense of what the product or service in question does, who it does that for, and what advantages the target company holds over the competition.

It bears repeating: This isn't merely something for sales or marketing people to master. These days, market orientation is something employers want to cultivate in all employees at all levels.

Message number 3: *You must pass along success stories that demonstrate your **market orientation and product/service knowledge,** even if you are not applying for a sales or marketing position.*

Don't be misled by the name or department associated with the position you're applying for. A working knowledge of the target company's products and services, as well as an understanding of its customer base, is essential in today's employment market.

You should be able to discuss, at the drop of a hat, new ways the company might market its products and services. Perhaps more importantly, you should be able to cite examples from your own background in which you dealt well with customers and prospective customers. Here are three examples of what your stories might sound like.

Once a decision was made, I did not worry about it afterwards.

—Harry S. Truman

More success stories

"As part of a research project I was working on for my boss, I had to interview potential customers for a new product the company was considering launching. The feedback I passed along from the people I spoke with turned out to be essential to the success of the product. I found out later that the interviews I conducted helped to identify three or four potentially serious design flaws."

ᔕ ᔕ ᔕ ᔕ ᔕ

"Once, at my previous job, there was a scheduling error, and there were no front-desk people to man the phones for customer queries over the 800 line. This happened during the middle of a major national advertising campaign! I volunteered to help out, and it was a very positive experience all the way around. I had to learn on my feet, and the first few calls I had to ask for a little help from people,

but after about half an hour I got the hang of it. Fortunately, I was already familiar with the promotion and the product line."

᧞ ᧞ ᧞ ᧞ ᧞

"After graduating from college, I worked as a telemarketer for a time for a telecommunications firm. I did cold calls for a line of pocket pagers, and I sold quite a few of them. I didn't stay in the job for long because I found a job in a publishing setting that made more sense for me, but I did make Salesperson of the Month twice during my time there. I was kind of proud of that."

Important note: In today's employment environment, displaying market orientation to the prospective employer is vitally important, even (especially!) if your career experience and career objectives do not relate to marketing or sales. In addition to brief stories of the kind outlined here, you are well-advised to develop at least one extended story that shows your market orientation to the greatest advantage. When you finally schedule a face-to-face meeting with a decision-maker, and that person asks an appropriate question, you should offer your in-depth anecdote.

The anecdote should show how you overcame significant obstacles to post *respectable* (not necessarily spectacular) results when called upon to deal with customers or potential customers. Here's an example:

"I can't claim to have much of a sales background, and I've never worked as a salesperson officially, as far as job descriptions go, but I did have a fascinating experience along these lines that may be

worth discussing. I once had to fill in when three of my company's top people came down with the flu...right before an extremely important trade show.

"As a general rule, this event represented something like 30 percent of the company's annual business, so people were a little worried when the president, the vice president of marketing, and the vice president of marketing's assistant all got so sick that they couldn't make the trip. The job of manning the booth and asking for orders fell to me and to the president's personal assistant—and neither of us had ever attended this trade show before! We got a telephone briefing from the president—who sounded really, really sick—and a brief set of written instructions from the vice president of marketing. And that was it. We had one day to prepare and we spent most of it memorizing names from the company address book—names of people we were likely to meet.

"At the end of the day, the office manager handed us a couple of airline tickets and wished us luck. We did some role-playing exercises on the plane, and we kept it up that night at the hotel.

" The first day of the show rolled around and we worked like dogs. The assistant and I showed up at 7 a.m., set up the exhibit, then took turns dashing to the restroom so we could change out of our work clothes and into our business suits! Well, the long and the short of it was that we did $262,000 worth of business over the three days of the show—which was about 90 percent of the amount the event usually generated. We thought that was pretty good for a couple of rookies."

Take a few moments now to consider what kind of interactions with customers or prospective customers may be the basis for a story along the lines of the one here. Remember, your objective is not to demonstrate that you achieved superior sales results. It's not even to prove that you closed a sale—although if you have a story like this one you should certainly provide all the details! Instead, the in-depth story you develop should outline a time when you had to deal directly with the people who actually used and/or bought the product or service your company provided...and it should show, in a compelling fashion, exactly how you kept them happy.

If you ever sold something, resolved a customer's problem, kept a dissatisfied patron from going to the competition or resolved a potentially disastrous miscommunication between someone in the organization and a customer or potential customer, you can—and should—develop an in-depth story to communicate your market orientation.

Just to review...

You will want to use the ideas that follow in this book to demonstrate specifically that:

- You are adaptable and deal well with change.

- You know that efficiency and bottom-line results are essential.

- You have a good sense of the organization's products and/or services, and you could, if you had to, explain what the company has to offer in a compelling way to a prospective customer.

As you look over the list, you may find yourself wondering: Aren't the things you're offering to provide to the employer—the ability to manage change well, the ability to deliver results efficiently and profitably, and a sense of marketing flair—aren't those the very same problems your *superiors* are supposed to be keeping an eye out for? Aren't the managers the ones whose job it is to instruct people in taking on unexpected duties? Turning their attentions to profitable activity? Thinking about competitive advantage, customers and sales? After all, if these problems don't fall within the formal, written duties of the job you're after, why should you prepare yourself to address them?

Today's economic and business realities demand that you become, to a certain extent, *your own manager*. That's the often-overlooked implication of all this downsizing and short-staffing that's been going on in our economy. When employers *do* decide to take on new people, they do so, more and more, because they think the hires have a good chance of working out well *on their own,* with as little watering and maintenance as possible.

> *You gain strength, courage and experience by every experience in which you really stop to look fear in the face.*
> —Eleanor Roosevelt

It's a fact. If you want to look like everyone else—and get rejected like everyone else—then you don't have to worry about the three messages we just examined. You can act as though it's always the manager's responsibility to take care of adaptations to new technologies, bottom-line concerns and interactions with prospective customers. If, on the other hand, your aim is *to get hired in short order,* you'll need to prove to the employer that he or she has hooked up with someone who can deliver results in a work environment where supervisory or managerial resources are scarce.

The competitors for the job you want can fret about written job descriptions, formal lines of authority and other relics of the employment world of yesterday. You are trying to get a job today. Your success stories, then, must broadcast the right messages for today's employment realities.

Seize the opportunity by the beard; it is bald from the rear.
—Bulgarian proverb

You're not done yet

You'll be using your success stories again and again, so you should eventually memorize their details and be prepared to recite them at a moment's notice. However, because your job search is going to be an accelerated one, you will need much more information than these stories. The specifics of your job history must be able to match up, and quickly, with the specific requirements of the employer. That means developing a solid written file reflecting your job history before you contact anyone, a file you'll use when the prospective employer, piqued by your success stories, wants to hear more. Before you move on to the tasks of developing or expanding your target list of potential employers, or contacting them directly to share your success stories with them, there is one more piece of "self-research" for you to undertake.

Not only do I knock 'em out, I pick the round.
—Muhammad Ali

The questionnaires on pages 31 to 37 appear in Ron Fry's excellent book *101 Great Answers to the Toughest Interview Questions,* which is easily the finest published work available on the subject of interview preparation. Answer all the questions that follow before you proceed any further in this book. As you do so, please bear in mind that the more appropriate research work you do up front—both with regard to yourself *and* the prospective employer—the greater your ability to send a *customized* message will be, and the faster your job search will conclude successfully.

(The questionnaires, adapted from Ron Fry's *101 Great Answers to the Toughest Interview Questions* [Career Press, 1996] are reprinted by permission.)

You miss 100 percent of the shots you don't take.

—Wayne Gretzky

Employment data input sheet

Prepare a separate sheet for every full-time and part-time job you've ever held, no matter how short the tenure. Yes, even summer jobs are important here. They demonstrate resourcefulness, responsibility and initiative—that you were already developing a sense of independence while you were still living at home. For each employer, include:

- Name, address and telephone number.
- The names of all your supervisors and, whenever possible, where they can be reached.
- Letter of recommendation, if they cannot be reached.
- The exact dates (month/year) you were employed.

For each job, include:

- Your specific duties and responsibilities, such as "financial responsibilities" and "purchasing authority."

- Supervisory experience, noting the number of people you supervised.

- Specific skills required for the job.

- Your key accomplishments.

- The dates you received promotions.

- Any awards, honors and special recognition you received.

For each part-time job, add the number of hours you worked per week.

Don't write a book on each job. But do concentrate on providing specific data.

Great minds have purposes, others have wishes.

—Washington Irving

Volunteer work data input sheet

Take some time to make a detailed record of your volunteer pursuits, similar to the one you've just completed for each job you've held.

For each volunteer organization, include:

- Name, address and telephone number.

- The name and address of your supervisor or the director of the organization.

- Letter of recommendation.
- The exact dates (month/year) of your involvement with the organization.

For each volunteer experience, include:

- The approximate number of hours you devoted to the activity each month.
- Your specific duties and responsibilities.
- Specific skills required.
- Accomplishments.
- Any awards, honors and special recognition you received.

Awards and honors data input sheet

List all the awards and honors you've received from schools, community groups, church groups, clubs, and so on. You may include awards from prestigious high schools (prep schools or professional schools) even if you're in graduate school or long out of college

Other

You should also list any appropriate information reflecting hobbies, extracurricular activities, military service and foreign language ability.

Without completing these input sheets, the ideas that follow in this book will not work for you as well as they should, and you will probably *not* get the job offer you deserve in the time frame you desire.

EMPLOYMENT DATA INPUT SHEET

Employer Name: _____

Address: _____

Address: _____

Phone: _____

Dates of Employment: _____ to _____

Hours Per Week: _____ Salary/Pay: _____

Supervisor's Name and Title: _____

Duties: _____

_____

_____

_____

Skills Utilized: _____

_____

_____

_____

Accomplishments/Honors/Awards: _____

_____

_____

Other Important Information: _____

_____

_____

VOLUNTEER WORK DATA INPUT SHEET

Organization Name: _____

Address: _____

Address: _____

Phone: _____ Hours Per Week: _____

Dates of Activity: _____

Supervisor's Name and Title: _____

Duties: _____

_____

_____

_____

Skills Utilized: _____

_____

_____

_____

Accomplishments/Honors/Awards: _____

_____

_____

Other Important Information: _____

_____

_____

_____

HIGH SCHOOL DATA INPUT SHEET

School Name: _____

Address: _____

Phone: _____ Years Attended: _____

Major Studies: _____

GPA/Class Rank: _____

Honors: _____

Important Courses: _____

_____

_____

OTHER SCHOOL DATA INPUT SHEET

School Name: _____

Address: _____

Phone: _____ Years Attended: _____

Major Studies: _____

GPA/Class Rank: _____

Honors: _____

Important Courses: _____

_____

_____

COLLEGE DATA INPUT SHEET

College: _____

Address: _____

Phone: _____ Years Attended: _____

Degrees Earned: _____ Major: _____

Minor: _____ Honors: _____

_____

Important Courses: _____

_____

_____

GRADUATE SCHOOL DATA INPUT SHEET

College: _____

Address: _____

Phone: _____ Years Attended: _____

Degrees Earned: _____ Major: _____

Minor: _____ Honors: _____

_____

Important Courses: _____

_____

_____

ACTIVITIES DATA INPUT SHEET

Club/Activity: _____

Office(s) Held: _____

Description of Participation: _____

_____

Duties/Responsibilities: _____

_____

Club/Activity: _____

Office(s) Held: _____

Description of Participation: _____

_____

Duties/Responsibilities: _____

_____

AWARDS & HONORS DATA INPUT SHEET

Name of Award, Citation, etc.: _____

From Whom Received: _____

Date: _____ Significance: _____

_____

Other Pertinent Information: _____

_____

MILITARY SERVICE DATA INPUT SHEET

Branch: _____

Rank (at Discharge): _____

Dates of Service: _____

Duties and Responsibilities: _____

_____

_____

_____

Special Training and/or School Attended: _____

_____

_____

_____

_____

Citations, Awards, etc.: _____

_____

_____

_____

Specific Accomplishments: _____

_____

_____

_____

_____

LANGUAGE DATA INPUT SHEET

Language: _____

        ❏ Read   ❏ Write   ❏ Converse

Background (number of years studied, travel, etc.): _____

_____

_____

_____

Language: _____

        ❏ Read   ❏ Write   ❏ Converse

Background (number of years studied, travel, etc.): _____

_____

_____

_____

Language: _____

        ❏ Read   ❏ Write   ❏ Converse

Background (number of years studied, travel, etc.): _____

_____

_____

_____

_____

If you've completed the questionnaires, you're probably thinking about additions and changes you could make to the success stories you developed a little earlier. Don't worry—that's exactly what you *should* be thinking!

The success stories you develop in each of the three critical ability areas are so important that they deserve another look. Now that you've reviewed your entire work history, go back to the success stories and review them closely. Are there other incidents that do a better job of demonstrating your ability to deal well with change, your profit orientation, and your ability to assume a sales/marketing mindset? Is there a better way of phrasing a story you're confident gets the point across?

Take a few minutes now to review your success stories closely and make all appropriate revisions. Once you do, you'll be ready to move on to the next chapter.

People who believe they're going to have good luck and find the answer usually do find it because they've put the idea of their success into their subconscious.

—Bill Lear

Chapter 2

The people you'll contact

So—once you've developed a target company list, who, specifically, do you tell your success stories to? And how do you reach that person?

To be a success in business, be daring, be first, be different.

—Marchant

Getting the right job quickly means talking to the right people

You can, of course, follow the "traditional" advice and contact your target organization's personnel or human resources department. Be forewarned that you'll probably be met with the traditional roadblocks from these folks who reject job-seekers for a living. That's what they spend most of their day doing. That's what they're trained to do. So that's probably—not definitely, but *probably*—what they're going to do when they hear your success story.

This is a book about getting the right results from the job search process *fast*. So the advice it offers is not in any way traditional. This book's guiding principles, when it comes to targeting your success stories, are as follows:

- Avoid any contact with human resource and personnel offices for as long as you can.

- Contact the very highest person possible within the organization *first*. Allow that person to tell you what to do. Follow these instructions carefully and to the letter. Follow up appropriately by phone or fax with updates after making contact.

- Ignore formal application procedures unless they are laid out for you by the person who would actually be supervising you on the job, or by the head of the organization.

- When told there are no openings for you, call back on an aggressive *yet excruciatingly polite* follow-up schedule, regardless of what you are told about the company's hiring timelines. (Hey, people quit unexpectedly, don't they?)

In other words—when in doubt, call the president of the company personally to share your success story, and follow up tenaciously but with unfailing politeness thereafter.

You read right. To get the right results fast, you will need to develop a studious obliviousness for the organization's formal hiring procedures. Instead, you will present yourself as someone who has something important to offer to the *president or chief executive officer* of the company. That's what the top person's son- or daughter-in-law would do, right? If it's good enough for family, it's good enough for you.

> *Optimists do not wait for improvement; they achieve it.*
> —Paul von Keppler

Sales trainer Tony Parinello, whose superb book *Selling to the Very Important Top Officer* outlines a straight-to-the-top approach for the world of sales, points out that CEOs and the like love to give orders. That's what *they* do all day long. So you're going to let them tell you what to do. Parinello also accurately notes that the *second* most important person in the organization is often the CEO's personal assistant!

Specific techniques for dealing with the topmost people in an organization, both in person and on the phone, will follow shortly. For now, take a moment to review the following important principles.

- This is a free country. You can pick up the phone and call anyone you want. The IRS will not start following you around if you call the president of the company you want to work for and ask for a job, nor will you lose your eligibility to compete in the Olympics.

- The head of the organization may be the one person in the company who is *always* on the lookout for opportunity. That's why it's worth taking the trouble to get in touch with him or her.

- Talking with CEOs (and other top-level people in the organization) may take a little persistence, but it doesn't actually *hurt*. (The conversations, good or bad, are usually over in an instant.) Talking with *lots* of CEOs, and letting them refer you to others in the organization, is the best possible way to get the job offer you deserve.

- Some of the older, stodgier industries and companies may put significant roadblocks between you and the president. But can they fault you for trying? At the very least, you may be able to develop some high-powered referrals. Remember to try to make an ally out of the president's assistant. Where can he or she point you?

"What's our next step?"

Your ability to project a positive, confident persona while delivering your success story tells the employer some very important things about you. You are polite, but persistent; you know how to take charge; you handle potentially stressful situations well.

At the conclusion of your story, you're going to have another opportunity to demonstrate these important, desirable traits—and another one, the ability to *do what it takes to get results from the organization*—by confidently asking the following question. I strongly advise that you pose it exactly as it's laid out below:

Mr. / Ms. Bigshot, let me ask your advice. What do you think I need to do to get a chance to work for your organization right away—and show you how I can start delivering results?

This question may well turn a brush-off into a job interview. I recommend that you pose it at the conclusion of any conversation with a decision-maker that does *not* result in a specific "here's-the-person-you-should-call" referral. When you are speaking face-to-face with the person, look your contact straight in the eye and pose the question as I have outlined it. (This may take some practice. Enlist the aid of a family member for some role-playing work before you try this on a real, live employer.)

As you will be reminded throughout this book, the question just outlined represents a superb way to end an in-person interview.

Damn the torpedoes. Full speed ahead.
—David Glasgow Farragut's shipboard order to
besieged Union navy men at Mobile Bay

The power of the telephone

Your telephone represents the single most powerful weapon in your get-the-right-job-fast arsenal. It allows you to call important decision-makers (including CEOs and the like) on *your* terms, according to *your* schedule and with *your* objective.

The only reliable way to get the job you deserve on an aggressive schedule is to *change the dynamic of your job search.* Using your telephone as the primary tool, you must change your job search mindset from a passive state, in which you wait for people to tell you what the status of your application is, to a proactive marketing campaign in which *you* more or less run the show.

Opportunities are seldom labeled.
—John A. Shedd

This doesn't mean being arrogant or inconsiderate on the phone. On the contrary, you must observe the most scrupulous courtesy with *all* the people you come in contact with at the target organization. *That includes the support staff at all levels!* Don't torpedo your job search campaign by coming on like El Fascisto to the receptionist, then turning into a sweetness-and-light machine when the decision-maker comes on the line. Your tone must be polite, directed and persistent. Persistence is indeed what counts the most on the job front, but it can be instantly undercut if you come across as arrogant, elitist or ill-mannered in your calls.

> *Persistent calling*
> + *Success stories*
> + *Poise in the face of adversity*
> = *People on the other line concluding they should have you on their side.*

> *Persistent calling*
> + *Success stories*
> + *Frustration, anger or stress*
> = *People on the other line wondering "when that jerk is going to leave us alone."*

Here's an example of the way your phone contacts with a particular target employer might sound over a period of days. Because you'll be making many calls to many target employers, you must keep a written or computerized log of your calls. See page 115 for an example of what such a log might look like.

Day one

Receptionist: *Bigshot Industries.*
You: *Leslie Bigshot's office, please.*
Receptionist: *One moment, please.*

Note: Asking the receptionist confidently for your target person will usually, but not always, connect you to the person's office. Sometimes you will reach the target person's personal assistant. *This is a step forward, not a roadblock.* Take down the assistant's name in your logbook when he or she answers the phone.

Assistant: *Leslie Bigshot's office, this is Brian speaking.*
You: *Hi, Brian, this is Jane Jobseeker calling.*

Move directly into your success story. Both the decision-maker and his or her personal assistant are good people to share this story with. On the telephone, you may find that endorsement-related stories win the most interest.

You: *Mark Bossman of ABC Corporation called me "the star of the department" and said my technical reports had saved his division—and I'm quoting here, "at least $20,000 in the first quarter of 1996." Unfortunately, ABC is undergoing a downsizing campaign this year, and I am on the list to be let go by June 1. Brian, I'm calling today to ask Ms. Bigshot about opportunities for engineers at Bigshot Industries. Is she in today?*

If you deliver your *brief* success story in this way, and then ask to speak directly to your target person, you will often be presented with one of three positive outcomes:

1. Brian will put you through directly to Ms. Bigshot. (It happens, so be ready to repeat your success story and ask for an interview with her.)
2. Brian will tell you a good time to call Ms. Bigshot.
3. Brian will refer you to the person with hiring authority in the area of interest to you. This counts as a plus!

Remember, the assistant to the top person in the organization is often among the most important players in the company, flow chart or no flow chart. Use the assistant's name when you contact the decision-maker.

Sometimes, of course, you'll hear something like this:

Assistant: *Ms. Bigshot is going to be busy all day today. Can I take your number and have her get back to you?*

Surprise, surprise. As a very general rule, people at the very top of the organization are better about returning their calls—or having someone else return them—than just about anyone else. Still, you're more likely to get further if you leave a personal message, so try this:

You: *That's a great idea. Can I leave a message on her voice mail?*

Assistant: *Sure. Hold on.*

If there is no voice mail system, or if the assistant is hesitant about connecting you to the voice mailbox, politely leave your number and move on to the next target employer. Otherwise:

> Ms. Bigshot's voice: *Hi, you've reached Leslie Bigshot. I'm not in at the moment, but if you leave your name and number, I'll get back to you.*

> You: *Hi, Ms. Bigshot. Mark Bossman of ABC Corporation called me "the star of the department" and said my technical reports had saved his division—and I'm quoting here, "at least $20,000 in the first quarter of 1996." Unfortunately, ABC is undergoing a downsizing campaign this year, and I am on the list to be let go by June 1. This is Jane Jobseeker. I'm calling today to ask about opportunities for engineers at Bigshot Industries. Could you please give me a call back at 617-555-1234? Thanks!*

Important note: You are likelier to reach Mr./Ms. Bigshot in person if you call early in the morning or some time after 5 p.m. If you can elicit Mr./Ms. Bigshot's phone extension from the receptionist or anyone else, you'll be able to bypass the phone system and get to your decision-maker while he or she is putting in a little workaholic time. If you *don't* have the direct number, read on.

Day two

This is a book about how to get the right job *fast,* so we're going to place the default setting on your Magic Telephone Follow-up Machine at "one business day plus an hour or so." That is to say, if you leave a message at 4 p.m. on Friday, you can feel comfortable calling your target person back first thing Tuesday morning. Here's an example of what your conversation might sound like:

Last Minute Job Search Tips

Receptionist: *Bigshot Industries.*

You: *Brian in Leslie Bigshot's office, please.*

Thanks to your last call, you now have someone to ask for. Thanks to your unfailing politeness to Brian the last time around, he'll be a pretty good bet to help you track down your target person.

Receptionist: *One moment....*

Brian: *Leslie Bigshot's office.*

You: *Hi Brian. Jane Jobseeker. We spoke yesterday about the $20,000 I saved ABC Corporation. I was just calling to see if Ms. Bigshot was free to talk about what I could do for your organization.*

Brian: *Right—I know she got your message—can you hold on for a moment?*

You: *Sure. (Pause.)*

Ms. Bigshot: *Leslie Bigshot here.*

Don't launch into the same story! Offer another one.

You: *Ms. Bigshot, thanks for taking the call. Over at ABC Industries, I worked on a very complex product-development project that was budgeted to take 90 days—I brought it in in 67, and our head of Quality Control told me it was the sharpest job he'd ever seen. As you may know, there's a downsizing campaign underway at ABC right now, and my job is scheduled to be eliminated on June 1. What I'd like to do is come by for a brief meeting with you to talk about what I could offer Bigshot Industries. Is Tuesday at 10 a.m. a good time for you?*

Yes, you should really end by specifying a time for the interview!

Once you have done so, stop talking and wait to hear what the decision-maker has to say. More often than you'd expect, you'll hear, "Well, Tuesday's full—could you come by Thursday?"

But suppose you hear something like this:

Ms. Bigshot: *Why don't you send a resume along and let me (or our Human Resources Department) take a look at it?*

You: *That's a great idea. Just so I can get an idea of what you're trying to get accomplished at your company these days, Ms. Bigshot, let me ask you something: What's the main thing you look for when hiring new employees in this area?*

Ask about "new employees in this area" rather than "engineers" (or whatever your specialty is) because you want to get one of Ms. Bigshot's abiding passions down in your notebook. You will then compose your resume around this element—and send a copy to both Ms. Bigshot and whomever she refers you to.

Day three (or later)

This is the tricky one. You've already had some kind of direct contact with Mr./Ms. Bigshot—now you have to decide how to proceed. If you've been ordered to contact someone in the organization, you can (and must) do so on the strength of your referral from Mr./Ms. Bigshot. If you haven't gotten such a referral, you may want to consider pursuing a third-time call *with the utmost politeness* and with due respect for the decision-maker's time. If Mr./Ms. Bigshot begins to perceive that you are a waste of time, your call will not be a productive one.

Last Minute Job Search Tips

The following sample dialogue assumes that you have crafted a targeted resume, one that focuses specifically on the position at hand and incorporates, perhaps in an unconventional way, on *only one or two* of your success stories.

Ms. Bigshot: *Leslie Bigshot here.*

You: *Ms. Bigshot, thanks for taking the time to talk to me. This is Jane Jobseeker. You'd asked me to send along my resume, and I wanted to make sure it got through all right.*

Because time was an issue, you sent the resume via the U.S. Postal Service's Priority Mail. It delivers your resume affordably, and with high impact—usually in only a day or two when you mail within your delivery area. *Don't call before the resume is likely to have arrived.*

Ms. Bigshot: *Yes, Jane, it came through, but to be honest I've only looked at it briefly. It did seem interesting, though.*

An opening. Resumes and cover letters that have an unconventional look to them, or focus tantalizingly on the details of one or two of your success stories, are the likeliest to generate a response like this. Try for an interview again.

You: *Ms. Bigshot, I know you're very busy, but I'd like to stop by for a brief meeting to discuss how I can help your engineering work at Bigshot Industries. Would Friday at 9 a.m. be all right?*

Again, you must ask directly for a specific time slot if you hope to accelerate the process. If you get a brush-off, *politely but firmly* pose the Next Stage question, outlined earlier in this chapter, and then *stop talking.*

Ms. Bigshot: *I really think you'd be better off talking to the Human Resources people, Jane.*

You: *Ms. Bigshot, let me ask your advice. What do you think I need to do to get a chance to work for your organization right away—and show you how I can start delivering results?*

If you ask this question slowly, confidently, and with a sense of purpose, a good many of the people you talk to will drop the barriers and begin to ask you about your background—or set up an interview on the spot.

No, sir. Because I have time to think before I speak, and don't ask impertinent questions.
—Erasmus Darwin, responding to a question concerning whether his stammering was an inconvenience

10 job search commandments for good phone presentations

The best books I have ever read on the topic of handling yourself on the phone are Stephan Schiffman's *Cold Calling Techniques (That Really Work!)* and Tony Parinello's *Selling to the Very Important Top Officer,* both of which should be available through your local bookstore. If you're interested in making the best possible presentation on the phone during your job search campaign, you owe it to yourself to review the ideas in these books. In the meantime, here are some basic points you should bear in mind as you make your calls.

First commandment:
Don't sound like a robot

Even the sharpest telemarketing strategy in the world isn't likely to do you much good if it sounds like you're reading a script word-for-word from a book. (This one, for instance.) Practice with a tape recorder until your success stories sound fluid and natural in the delivery.

Second commandment:
Refer to your results, not yourself

Some use of the words "I" and "my" are inevitable during a job search phone campaign. All the same, you should bear in mind that because the decision-maker has no experience or knowledge of you, appealing to the personal pronoun over and over isn't going to win you any points. Again, use a tape recorder to rehearse your presentation, and keep an ear out for overuse of "I" and "my"—a common problem in phone presentations.

Third commandment:
Instill some mystery, hold back details

The objective on the phone is to *get the other person to agree to a meeting,* not to get a job offer! Save some ammunition for that meeting. Keep the person on the other end of the line wondering about exactly how you managed to do what you did.

Fourth commandment:
Avoid phone interviews

Dirty little secret: The reason a manager will try to go over your work history in detail by phone is to *eliminate you from consideration.* From a manager's perspective, shortening the list by phone is preferable to doing so in person. It may feel flattering to have all those questions pointed your way, but your candidacy will probably stand a better chance of resulting in a job offer if you give a brief answer, then press tactfully, but firmly, for a time that you and the decision-maker can get together in person.

Fifth commandment:
Interpret "Send me a resume" to mean...

"Send me a resume and then follow up appropriately by phone." It can't be overstated: Making polite, persistent telephone contact at all points of the process is the single best way to better your odds on the job search front. Whenever possible, send a *targeted* resume that directly addresses the challenges of the position in question. Supply tantalizing details from *one or two* of your success stories. Leave a lot to the imagination; you can supply the details at the interview.

Sixth commandment:
Back it all up with third-party referrals

For each of your success stories, you should, if humanly possible, arrange for a credible third party to serve as an instant, on-the-spot endorsement for the anecdote you've just passed along. That way, when someone asks you over the phone about your references, you have an alternative to simply supplying the name and number and waiting for a week or two. You can say, "Why don't I do this—George Freeman, who was my supervisor and worked with me on the project, has told me he's willing to serve as a telephone reference. May I have him call you this morning?"

Seventh commandment:
Don't carry frustration to the next call

Let's face it. Calling means hearing *no* over and over again. (See the section on the *numbers game* on page 55.) Nevertheless, it's worth remembering that the person you're calling now has nothing to do with—and knows nothing about—what just happened to you on the phone. If you have any doubt about your ability to approach the next call with a *completely* positive attitude, take a break. This book will frequently remind you of the importance of observing this often-violated command.

Eighth commandment:
Don't make calls all day long

Calling is essential work, but it can also be quite stressful. Professional salespeople may be comfortable making cold calls for long periods of time, but the rest of us are likely to benefit from a change of pace and/or scenery.

Ninth commandment:
Do a little every day

Until you land in the job that's right for you, cold calling is not something you can get "out of the way." It should be an ongoing part of your job search campaign. I recommend that you devote a solid hour to 90 minutes of each day to job-search related cold calling, *no matter how well things are going on other fronts*. If you don't have a formal, on-the-table offer from an employer you want to work for, you still need to make calls.

Tenth commandment:
Reward thyself

Cold calling is tough work. When you've completed your cold calls for the day, give yourself a reward of some kind, *regardless of whether you think the calls went well.* Play a favorite high-energy song. Eat a nonfattening snack. Call a friend who always makes you feel better. Watch a favorite video. If you made the calls and marked them in your log, you earned your reward.

> *The other day a man asked me what I thought was the best time of life. "Why," I answered without a thought, "now."*
> —David Grayson

The numbers game

Why do some people's job search campaigns seem to take forever?

Part of the reason has to do with an unfortunate willingness to take, at face value, various "expert opinions" as gospel when it comes to estimating the time necessary to find a better job. Someone reads that a high-profile outplacement firm somewhere has estimated that the "right" time to find a good job is one month for every $10,000 of salary. And that person concludes that the experts, who must know best, are right. So nothing happens for the next six months because nothing is "supposed" to happen. (Woe unto the person who earned $120,000 per year and now must find work! A year of waiting must precede any job offer!)

Your future is in *your* hands now, today, this minute. If you earned $60,000 per year and are now out of work, you *can* get work that's right for you...and quickly. (The rest of this book is filled with ideas that will help you do so.) You *do not* have to wait six months.

But having an idea of the numbers involved *is* helpful on the job front in a very limited, but nevertheless essential, sense. I'm going to go out on a limb here and estimate, based on my own experience in the world of sales—and as a hiring manager for more than 10 years—that you are going to have to talk to *25* decision-makers for every *one* who's likely to turn into a promising employment opportunity (typically, an in-person job interview). And for each *10* of those meetings you go on, you're likely to get *one* job offer.

Those numbers will vary from person to person and industry to industry, of course, and to many who are just starting out on the job search front, they may appear quite daunting. They're actually wonderful news—if *you* assume control of the cycle.

As you approach the full-time job of finding the right job for you, you must consider your job to be to hear no as often as possible, so that you can reduce the amount of time necessary to get to the yes waiting for you at the end of the line.

I propose to fight it out on this line if it takes all summer.

—General Ulysses S. Grant

In other words, you need to conscientiously, positively prospect in such a way that you get the first 24 no's *on the board*. (And even a no can serve to generate a valuable referral.) Then you can work on nailing that 25th call, the one with the interview attached to it. *The numbers do even out in the end.* The only sin is in failing to allow them to do so, or allowing the initial no's we receive to so cloud our perceptions that employers get a skewed perception of what type of employee we would make.

The reason so many job searches drag on forever is usually that the person conducting the search considers a no outcome to be a setback. In fact, no is just the opposite.

Things don't turn up in this world until someone turns them up.
—James A. Garfield

If you make three cold prospecting calls a day, you are probably at least a week away from setting up an interview. Can you afford that week? More to the point, can you afford the 80-plus business days—or four months—it's likely to take you to develop a single job offer?

If, on the other hand, you make 15 to 20 calls per day (and by "calls," I mean exchanges in which you talk to someone new who could conceivably set up an interview with you, not fencing matches with receptionists), you're probably only a day or two away from being able to schedule an interview with a solid prospective employer.

You read right. If you keep up a positive mental outlook, develop compelling success stories, aim high in the target organization and make persistent calls along the lines set out in this chapter, you can expect to set up an honest-to-goodness interview after only a day or two of calling. And if you keep up the routine—without getting sidetracked by your own success or disheartened by the 24 no's—you can expect to develop *multiple* job offers within a month.

Last Minute Job Search Tips

The single best way to get the job you deserve, *quickly*, is to contact the very topmost people in your target organizations, relay compelling success stories that take into account the qualities employers are looking for in today's economic environment, and keep it up, *no matter what happens,* every day. I suggest a minimum of 20 new contacts every day. (If you're trying to get a job more or less *instantly,* you'll want to up that total to at least 25.) If you follow this plan, which I've taken a full chapter to lay out for you, you should see results fast. If you let a few no's get you down, or decide you don't have to make calls today because you've got a promising interview scheduled for next week, then you probably won't see results fast.

Lots of other ideas for getting job offers are set out in the following chapters. Some offer specific variations on the regimen you've just read about; some take dramatically different approaches. All will benefit from your willingness to work the following principles into your job search.

- *Feel free to contact any employer who tells you no all over again after 10 days.* Some experts suggest that you wait 30 days to do this. That's nonsense. In today's economy, 10 days is an eternity. Entire markets can come into existence, or disappear, in 10 days. Develop new success stories. Call again. Be unfailingly polite at all times. See what happens. Consider "We don't have a position for you." to mean (as it does!) "We don't have a position for you *today.*"

- *Develop a true passion for the industry you want to enter or reenter.* If you don't have the "fire in the belly," that will show to prospective employers. If, on the other hand, you follow trends because you like to, and have *strong opinions about those trends*, you will stand out from other applicants. If you can't get obsessed about the industry you're trying to win a job in, find another industry to target!

- *Remember that the employer is buying your attitude as well as your skill set.* Find something that makes you happy. Whatever it is, incorporate it into your daily routine. Do not contact any employer, in person or via the telephone, when you are feeling depressed.

What you *think* during your prospecting efforts isn't background music. Instead, your mental attitude constitutes an ongoing series of instructions to yourself, a set of instructions with a profound impact on how you present your candidacy to prospective employers. This point is worth examining in some detail. Read on!

Your mindset is everything

The best advertisement likely to get you a good job quick? Simple. *Enjoy yourself, even when others wouldn't.* Most people like to run into individuals for whom life is a joy, not a chore. People who adopt, and *keep*, an optimistic mindset during the job search are more likely to secure the cooperation, advice and help of decision-makers.

Now, such suggestions are all very well in theory. The truth is, though, you're reading this book because you have to. You need to find work and you don't have long to wait to find it. Canvassing for job leads, you may be thinking to yourself, is serious business—and sometimes, it isn't much fun. All of that is certainly true.

But remember this: The very obstacles you face on the job search are "audition pieces" of sorts, hurdles you can turn to your advantage by treating them as opportunities to demonstrate your ability to handle tough situations and maintain your cool under fire.

When you come right down to it, your *upbeat reaction* to the circumstances you face is probably the single most important factor affecting the speed and success of your job search campaign.

Mishaps are like knives, that either serve us or cut us, as we grasp them by the blade or by the handle.
—James Russell Lowell

If the answer to your job search query is no, you *must* avoid the temptation to fall into a fault-finding or blaming mode. Instead, you should smile in a genuine, undaunted way and react as though the answer were "not right now, thanks, but keep trying." Keep the lines of communication open with the prospective employer and *politely* inform him or her that you'll be in touch again before too long to see if things have changed.

If the answer to your job search query is "not right now, thanks, but keep trying," you must avoid the temptation to ask, "Well, *when?*" Instead, you should smile in a genuine, undaunted way and say, "You bet I will." And then call 10 days later.

There's a country music song that points out the necessity of singing like you don't need the money. That sentiment should guide your every action as you plan your accelerated job search. Employers like to hire people who sing like they don't need the money. (And here's a bonus—as a general rule, employers like to pay them well, too.)

What you communicate to the prospective employer, verbally or on paper, is his or her best (and perhaps only) source of information about what you will be like to work with. *This means that a negative, overbearing or hostile reaction to a no answer will only serve to convince the employer that the right decision was made.* So what? Well, following up on your *rejections* may constitute your best statistical chance at landing a job—so there's no sense convincing anyone, at any time, that you aren't the right person to take on board! *Every* decision-maker you talk to should be accorded your best treatment. *Every* decision-maker you talk to should be treated as a "live" employment lead, no matter what you hear that seems to indicate the contrary.

The only decent way to get something done is
to get it done by someone who quite likes doing it.
—D.H. Lawrence

Take a little test right now. Let's pretend you're a manager with hiring authority. Which of these two personality types would *you* be more likely to want hanging around the office eight hours a day?

1. "Ms. Jones, let me level with you. I've got a family to feed. The wolf is at the door. If I can't start work with your company next week, I don't know what I'm going to do. I'll do anything...anything at all. I've simply got to get a job, and if I don't get one with you, I'm not sure what's going to happen to us."

2. "Ms. Jones, I've got some ideas about how you
   can dramatically increase sales in your division.
   The strategies I'm talking about helped me post
   a 15-percent quarterly increase when I was
   sales manager at ABC Company. Now that my
   daughter's in day care all day and I'm back in
   the job market, I'd like to talk about how I can
   implement them for you at your company on a
   full-time basis. Could we get together Tuesday
   at 2 p.m.?"

No contest, right? Unless you have an affinity for pain and
discomfort, you'd probably *much* rather talk to the second
person than the first. So would prospective employers.

*The moral is simple: Depression and desperation don't
sell—but poise and confidence do.*

Ready to roll?

Congratulations! You're now ready to make use of the
specific employer contact ideas in this book. As you start
your campaign in earnest, please bear in mind that getting
a job *fast* isn't always the same thing as getting the *right*
job fast. The stronger your sense of purpose, and the more
detailed your up-front research, the better your chances of
landing a job that really makes sense for you from a personal, financial and, yes, spiritual standpoint. Saying you'll
"do anything," as we have seen, isn't particularly appealing
to prospective employers—and it may just land you in a job
you end up leaving soon after starting.

Chapter 3

Techniques to help you get a job within 1 to 5 days

*A wise man will make more opportunities
than he finds.*

—Francis Bacon

The faster you want to get a job, the more important maintaining your positive mindset will be. When in doubt, focus on things you enjoy during your contacts with prospective employers.

If you feel yourself beginning to resent the 24 no's that come before the first yes, take a break. *Do not, under any circumstances, take your frustration out on the next person you come in contact with.* Stop. Do something you enjoy for at least five minutes. Return to your contact work when you are feeling optimistic once again.

Last Minute Job Search Tips

You have a right—and, during the job search process, a duty—to do at least one nice thing for yourself at least once a day. *If you don't follow this advice, you won't get the most you can from the ideas in this book.*

Be prepared to put in some long hours. If you're not presently pulling a paycheck, the most debilitating myth you will encounter is the one that sounds like this: "I don't have a job." *You do have a job!* Your job is now marketing yourself to prospective employers and generating job offers. You must exhibit the same professionalism, diligence and commitment to this job as you would to any other work-related assignment.

As a matter of fact, because you're reading this chapter, I'm going to assume that you are interested in generating job offers in an *extremely time-sensitive fashion.* That means, in all likelihood, working 12- to 14-hour days (stay away from the all-nighters), and incorporating advice that is appropriate for you in an extremely aggressive (yet always optimistic!) fashion.

Not everything that follows in this chapter will be right for you, but much of the advice you will read about here is applicable to virtually any job search campaign.

If at all possible, save clerical, research, mailing-related and administrative work for the hours when you cannot telephone or meet personally with prospective employers or the people who can refer you to them. Depending on your personal sleep and activity patterns, this may mean *either* doing this work in the hours before 8 a.m.—or doing this work after 6 p.m. or so.

You say you're holding down a full-time job down now, and you still want to make very rapid progress on the employment front? Unless you can string at least three or four vacation days together, you should realistically expect things to extend somewhat beyond the job-offer-in-a-week category. That said, you should make the most of that crucial lunch hour by picking and choosing from the following ideas that appeal most to you. If you can, enlist the aid of a friend or family member when it comes to proofreading *targeted* resumes and cover letters (a vital step) and sending off mailings.

Once again: If you want to see results in a hurry, clear the decks and *put the time in all day long.* Procrastination and delay are your real enemies, not the job market. The right job for you *is* out there...and by using the ideas in this chapter, you can accelerate the process of finding it.

A man can succeed at almost anything for which he has unlimited enthusiasm.
—Charles Schwab

Start your campaign

Contact 20 to 25 presidents of target organizations every day, no matter what, and ask each to set up a meeting with you for the next day. See Chapter 2 for detailed advice on conducting your top-level telemarketing campaign. Offer to show up after business hours if necessary. (Placing your calls early may be a good idea for getting around gatekeepers, especially if your research has led you to the decision-maker's direct extension.)

Important note: Some of the people you talk to will tell you no. Be ready for that. Remember that such responses do not diminish your status as a candidate, but actually bring you closer to the next yes. Keep at it, and you will hook up with people who will either agree to meet with you or provide important referrals within the organization. When you start having trouble making time for your calls because you've scheduled interviews, you'll know you're making progress. Your library research should lead you toward contact information for at least 125 target companies (preferably smaller, entrepreneurial ones) before you try this.

Prepare and rehearse your success stories thoroughly. Be prepared to inject them, tactfully, into the conversation at a moment's notice.

Don't forget that the Big Cheese's personal assistant is one of the most important players in the organization. Share your stories with him or her as well.

Let your hook always be cast. In the pool
where you least expect it, there will be fish.

—Ovid

Turn rejections into challenges

Keep a detailed file on every single rejection you've gotten thus far, and follow up *immediately* by phone and on paper with an incredibly polite thank-you message. Okay, okay, this might not help you get a job offer within five days—then again, it just might. I've heard of candidates who turned rejections into instant job offers by passing along the detailed strategic recommendations they'd developed as part of their application for the target company.

Then there are the candidates whose unfailing positive, personal touch made employers think twice about giving them the cold shoulder. (This type of approach can be particularly effective if the position you're after involves dealing with the public.)

Most candidates take rejection as a personal affront, and even grumble under their breath a bit about getting even with the prospective employer somehow. Don't be like them. All the employer has told you is that he or she is not interested in giving you a job *now*. Someone who takes the trouble to call or write to advise you of the status of your candidacy is someone who should be in your prospect base. Show 'em what you're made of. Keep in touch.

Do not pester the prospective employer. Do leave a brief, poised, polite thank-you message on the person's voice-mail system (first preference) or through a personal call (second preference). (Voice-mail messages have to be dealt with somehow, and they are usually reviewed at a time that's convenient for the prospective employer.

See the following advice on dealing with company voice-mail systems effectively. See the advice in later chapters on using rejections as high-quality prospecting leads.

I am unfaithful to my own possibilities when I await from a change of circumstances what I can do on my own initiative.

—Karl Jaspers

Don't skip the important stuff

The two powerful strategies just outlined—developing high-quality leads by contacting the target organization's top decision-makers directly, and making the most of the rejections that come your way through persistent, optimistic follow-up—should be considered *mandatory* steps for your accelerated job search campaign.

Pick and choose from what follows elsewhere in the chapter as you see fit, but do incorporate these two strategies in your canvassing efforts.

Plan to ponder:
Break the language barrier

Target a company that faces a language barrier in dealing with its customers. This is an idea you may want to consider if you did well in languages in school. Many companies and social service agencies—typically located in urban areas—must address the needs of customers and/or clients who do not speak English. When these employers find someone who can understand the current problems and concerns of people who speak Spanish, Korean, Vietnamese or some other foreign tongue, and who can relay the organization's response to those problems, they often hire them on the spot.

Don't say you're fluent in a language that you've only recently begun reviewing. By the same token, if you're a quick study, don't be afraid to make the most of your ability to get the main points across.

If you have a real facility with languages, you may be able to leap to the front of the line after spending only a few days with a taped home-study course. See what's available at your local library. Practice intensively with a friend or family member.

Where there are people, there are customers/clients, and where there are customers/clients, there are problems. The local phone company, employment office, social services agency, medical clinic, cable television provider or other organization that must deal the varied communities in your neighborhood may be very interested in you if you can help bridge the communications gaps they face.

The big thing is to do it.

—Kit Carson

Plan to ponder:
Make voice mail and fax your friends

Use the company voice-mail system to your advantage. This can be especially good advice if you are conducting a top-level telemarketing campaign as outlined previously. Remember, *voice mail is your friend.* As long as you know what you're going to say before you try to say it, you're in the driver's seat. You control the message and no one is trying to interrupt you.

Many of today's systems offer "directory functions" that will allow you to leave a message directly for the person you're targeting. Don't get hung up on titles. Don't talk about what *you* want. Simply share your success story with the voice-mail system and leave the prospective employer wanting to hear more. Withhold your name until the end of the message.

Practice the message beforehand. It could sound like this:

"Mr. Van Pelt, great to get through to you. When the people at ABC Accounting were facing a huge work backlog, they called on me to reorganize their filing system. Thanks to a new computer system that I implemented and trained people for, they were able to process payroll 24 percent more quickly, and with no

*drop in accuracy. Mr. Van Pelt, this is Jane Smith
calling. I can help solve your computer-system
problems and I'd like to talk to you about working at
your company. My number is 617-555-5432. Please
call when you get the chance, or I will return the call
tomorrow at 9 a.m."*

Keep the message brief. Enunciate. Make sure every word is clear.

Call back as you indicate, and if you reach the person's assistant, ask that person to outline what the organization is trying to get accomplished in your area of expertise. (Remember, assistants to bigshots are often some of the most important people in the organization!)

Use the company fax machine to your advantage. Wonderful news! Any number of potentially imposing obstacles fall by the wayside when you come into possession of a decision-maker's fax machine number. That assistant who thinks, mistakenly, that you're just like the other 150 people trying to get through on the phone, is no longer much of a factor. You can send the message at any time of the day or night, which can be a big plus if you're trying to keep your daytime hours open for direct telephone contact.

Perhaps most important of all, *you have complete control of your message and nobody is going to interrupt you.* As long as you keep things concise (one page maximum), focus on one of your success stories, and follow up appropriately by phone a day or so later. You really can't go wrong.

How do you get the number? Call the main number and say, "I'm trying to send a fax to John Smith. What number should I use?" If you get any static, give up and try again three or four hours later. Repeat as required. Follow up by telephone a day or so after you send your fax!

Don't be afraid to repeat the fax's success story verbatim when you reach the decision-maker by phone after sending your message. He or she will probably have an easier time remembering your story than your name.

Keep it brief! Keep it brief! Keep it brief! The point is worth emphasizing, because *people don't read long-winded letters in general,* and they don't read long-winded job application letters in particular. You have about three seconds of the decision-maker's attention to work with. Make the most of it.

These three things fill up all of human existence: work, will and success.
—Louis Pasteur

You say you don't have access to a fax machine—except for the Ripoff, Inc., outlet that charges you a dollar a page? I bet you do. If you can't get a friend to send the fax for you from his or her office, and you can't press your friendly neighborhood librarian into service—both excellent options when accompanied by equal measures of helpless, guilt-inducing pleading and doe-eyed innocence on your part—you still have an option. If you know someone who has a personal computer of recent vintage, odds are good these days that the system includes a modem and fax software. Promise to wash the person's car for the next six months or so if you can use the computer's fax feature during off hours.

Include all appropriate contact information in your fax.

Don't harass people. Sending repeated fax messages for hours on end ties up the company's lines and it probably won't win you any allies within the target organization

Important note: This technique isn't exactly *mandatory*, but I do recommend it very strongly. Intelligent, judicious use of the company's fax line is a *great* way to show off the research you've done, display your personal creativity and otherwise set yourself apart from the competition. Isn't technology wonderful?

Do what you can, with what you have, where you are.
—Theodore Roosevelt

Plan to ponder: Simply show up and start working

A risky undertaking, to be sure, but one well worth considering for the more adventurous—and, yes, skilled in the undertaking in question. In researching my book *303 Off-the-Wall Ways to Get a Job,* I tracked down stories of people who got jobs by: arriving with a throng of workers at the crack of dawn and convincing the foreman to hire them on the spot; walking into a crowded restaurant and pouring coffee to assist the overworked staff; and lying about the fact that they'd won the position in question! *I do not advocate that you engage in deception on the job front in any way,* but I do mention these stories as examples of what's possible to those who are brave enough to undertake some rather exceptional "job search" (job appropriation?) maneuvers. This option may be worth considering if you know what you're doing, if you have a winning smile and if you're feeling both a little brave *and* a little lucky.

The maneuver "you-might-as-well-hire-me-since-I'm-doing-a-great-job-for-you-already" is probably best filed under "Ways to find a stopgap job" or "Alternate income source in a big hurry." The gambit probably won't work that well for you if you're after a senior financial analyst position. (Although I would love for you to write me in care of the publisher if you manage to pull off this maneuver in a white-collar environment!)

Don't try this with something you are not good at already. The point you're trying to make with the manager is that you can make an *instant* contribution to the organization, not that you're severely in need of on-the-job training.

Genius is one percent inspiration and 99 percent perspiration.
—Thomas Edison

Plan to ponder:
Make a face-to-face appeal

Let me preface what follows with the following important information: *Trespassing on private property is illegal and you must not do it.* When someone asks you to leave private property that you didn't know *was* private property, do so. Now that we've gotten those important legal tips out on the table, it's worth noting that one of the best ways enterprising job seekers have found to get the right job fast is to, well, loiter persistently in appropriate places.

I've heard of people who got the job they wanted by standing next to the president's parking space before he showed up in the morning; by waiting to meet the decision-maker every morning at 6:30 for days on end; and by parking outside the facility overnight and keeping an eye out for the decision-maker, then exiting the car for an impromptu, on-the-spot interview. If you do this sort of thing in the wrong way, you're stalking. If you do it correctly, you're showing incredible persistence and determination. If you opt for this approach, be sure you fall into the latter category.

This technique probably should not constitute a major element of your job search campaign. If you decide to pursue it, do so in combination with other ideas in this book.

Depending on your attitude and that of the decision-maker you hook up with, this approach may deliver instant results. In other words, this method has a pretty good chance of letting you know exactly where you stand without having to wait around for a month before someone tells you the company's hiring intentions in your area of interest.

You should know, though, that the timelines involved can vary dramatically from one organization to another, and that some people will not react well to the technique. In short, this is a risky idea that *may* pay off instantly; hence its inclusion in this chapter. It should go without saying that you must be ready to recount your success stories at a moment's notice.

Once again: *If you're asked to leave the premises, do so.*

Plan to ponder:
Ask to see the president immediately

It sounds crazy, but it's worked!

Your best bet is to do a little research up front, and find a knowledge or skill gap in the president's background. (Following your industry's trade publications closely may point you toward this critical information.) If you can *help to fill that gap*, and if you can find a compelling way to get this point across to the president's assistant, you may stand a pretty good chance of pulling this off. Consider preceding your visit with a strategically designed fax message.

Obviously, you must be ready for an on-the-spot interview with the head honcho. Do your homework...in case the job search gods smile and give you what you want.

Plan to ponder:
Offer an ironclad guarantee

This works best with founders, entrepreneurs, CEOs and other bottom-line types, but it can deliver great results with others in the organization as well. Look the person right in the eye as the meeting draws to a close and say something along these lines: "Ms. Bigshot, I believe I can make a contribution here in short order, and I'm so certain of that that I'm willing to make you a guarantee. You let me start here tomorrow *(next week),* and I will, without fail, *(master the computer system) (close six sales) (increase your output in this department by 20 percent)* within one month. If I don't live up to your expectations, tell me, and I'll walk out the door with no hard feelings."

Sure, it takes a little nerve to say this. Sure, you have to deliver on your promise. But when applied with confidence and optimism, this technique is *highly likely to land you a job quickly.* That's what we're talking about, right?

Make a specific promise, preferably one that incorporates numbers. The more impressive the promise the better, of course—as long as it's one you can fulfill. Keep the one-month timeline for your probationary period—it's dramatic enough to win instant notice, and it helps the prospective employer feel that he or she is reducing the level of risk inherent in a new hire.

Work like a demon to hit the marks you've committed to during that first month! Once you've talked the talk, it's incumbent upon you to walk the walk.

Preparing for an interview? Take a look at this book's companion volume, *Last Minute Interview Tips*. Until then, remember to rehearse your success stories, and remember the magic words that can turn a phone contact into an interview—and an interview into a job.

Those magic words are as follows:

> *Mr. / Ms. Bigshot, let me ask your advice. What do you think I need to do to get a chance to work for your organization right away—and show you how I can start delivering results?*

೮᎓ ೮᎓ ೮᎓ ೮᎓ ೮᎓

If you've decided to undertake a realistic job search that has as its aim a solid job offer within five days, it's a pretty good bet that those five days are going to be busy (and interesting!). Make the most of them! Reach back and give this task your very best effort. Your work *will* pay off. And if, for whatever reasons, your timeline stretches out a little further, take a look at the ideas that follow in the later chapters of this book.

Chapter 4

Techniques to help you get a job within 6 to 10 days

So you have a *little* more time to land a job—but not much. Finding the right job is always a challenge, but moreso when you must find one fast. Just as in Chapter 3, you're advised to keep a positive outlook as you search for the job you must land in six to 10 days. Don't let the pressure turn you into an anxious, desperate individual or you'll have trouble convincing prospective employers that you'll be able to handle the stresses and pressures that come along with the job you're seeking.

With a few additional days to land your job, you're not as pressed to make as many contacts per day. But it's wise to contact at least 10 to 15 presidents of target organizations every day. Ask each to set up a meeting with you for the next day. See the advice in Chapter 2 for tips on strategizing your top-level telemarketing campaign.

Your library research should lead you toward contact information for at least 125 target companies (preferably smaller, entrepreneurial ones) before you try this.

The world belongs to the enthusiast who keeps cool.

—William McFee

Plan to ponder:
Use your rejection file as a lead source

Has it been 10 days since you contacted an employer who rejected your candidacy? If so, contact the person again, preferably by means of *polite* messages on both the company fax machine and the company voice-mail system.

Respect the prospective employer's time. Do not come across as overbearing or desperate. *Do* come across as confident, persistent and professional. See Chapter 3 for advice on using the target company's voice-mail system and fax machine to your advantage.

Important: If you are not keeping a detailed file of all your rejections and following up on them regularly, you are not making the most of the resources at your disposal. Your rejection file is one of the most important sources of employment leads you can track down—and the bigger it gets, the more likely you are to hook up with an employer who will take note of your persistence and your abilities.

In addition to contacting top decision-makers directly and making the best possible use of your rejection file—two ideas that, taken together, constitute the best general how-to advice when it comes to getting the right job in a hurry—you may want to review the other job search techniques described in Chapter 3.

Consider the advice about contacting top people and treating your rejections as employment-market gold to be *mandatory* if you expect to get the right job within an aggressive time frame. Consider the advice in the previous chapter to be *optional*. The advice you find there is targeted toward those interested in securing employment a little more quickly than the timeline addressed in this chapter, but you may want to adapt an idea from the earlier chapters of the book for use in your own accelerated employment campaign.

Send a customized mailing piece that prominently incorporates the company's logo, brochure or catalog. In other words, track down a brochure, flier or sales circular, and turn it into your stationery. By making an envelope out of the circular, or pasting bits of it onto your resume to highlight particular text points, you will instantly distinguish yourself from the other applicants for the position.

Follow up by telephone appropriately and be prepared to remind your contact person of your innovative approach. ("I was the one who built my resume around your 'Searching for the Best' advertisement—and I'd like to think that you just might have found it with me, Ms. Jones.")

Try to incorporate a single compelling idea that ties your materials to the organization's promotional piece. Examples might include:

"Your new hotel offers top-of-the line service to its guests—and I'm eager to help you maintain bottom-line solidity in the accounting department."

Or:

"Your recent annual report's theme, Serving the World One Customer at a Time, is in keeping with my personal commitment to deliver solid, detail-oriented sales results—one customer at a time. By maintaining a personalized approach with my customers, I was able to win Salesperson of the Year honors two years running at ABC corporation. Let's get together to talk about how I can deliver happy customers to you...one at a time."

Plan to ponder:
Submit your job-search battle plan

In other words, show exactly how you would prioritize, allocate scarce resources and direct customer outreach efforts *on the job* by submitting a detailed project outline that specifies how you plan to prioritize, allocate scarce resources and direct outreach efforts to *prospective employers*—right now!

Outline a specific, tangible objective at the beginning of your plan. ("Obtain a salaried position in a design-related capacity with a top engineering firm within 75 miles of New York City.") Then outline, in detail, all the steps you plan to take, or are taking, to reach that goal. Specify your backup and contingency plans, as well.

Your "project plan" should be specific to the particular employer you submit it to. In other words, it should emphasize parallels with whatever challenges you are likely to face on the job with that particular company.

Neatness counts! Your plan should be proofread carefully *by someone else*, and bound in an attractive way. A sharp packaging effort here can make all the difference.

This type of "reflective project"—a specific example of your own planning style that focuses not on some fictional, abstract or unfamiliar project, but on *you*—is a time-tested way to get employers to sit up and take notice. Executed properly and with sufficient care and research, it can deliver great results when adapted to a number of prospective employers in turn.

Leave a copy of your customized resume on the windshield of the president's car during the day. Isn't it convenient how many companies will set up their company parking lots in such a way as to allow you to identify exactly where the president will park? Actually, in researching my book, *303 Off-the-Wall Ways to Get a Job,* I ran into some stories that involved perching oneself *at* the parking space and waiting for the president to show up—then launching into an in-person sales pitch! That may (or may not) be a little overbearing for your tastes. If you try the hanging-out-by-the-parking-space approach, you should be careful to avoid turning your job search campaign into a standoff with security people. If you're asked to leave, do so.

You say the resume-on-the-windshield technique is more your style? Can't say I blame you. Remember to weave a *succinct* success story into your written presentation and to customize your resume to the needs and demands of the specific employer. Follow up appropriately by phone a day or so later.

Plan to ponder:
Develop an unignorable resume

While researching my book, *303 Off-the-Wall Ways to Get a Job,* I learned about people who blew their resumes up until they were three feet tall, then overnighted them to the prospective employer; people who printed their resume on the backs of product wrappers associated with the target company's product or service; and people who attached their resumes to the interiors of the boxes that held the evening pizza the company bigwigs intended to eat while burning the midnight oil!

Unconventional resumes and resume delivery systems *may* just move you to the front of the line. But remember, you must still do all the appropriate company research, target your resume directly to the challenges the organization faces, broadcast your appropriate success stories and leave some information to go over at the interview.

Be creative, but bear in mind that a gimmick employed for its own sake is unlikely to win you a job. Tie your message to the decision-maker's desire to run the business more efficiently, increase revenues and win new long-term customers. Stay away from offensive, off-color or insensitive messages in your resume and cover letter. If you go the pizza-box route (and many have), coat your resume in clear plastic. You don't want to get sauce on your credentials.

Vast is the primary power of the creative; all things owe to it their beginning.
                                                    —The *I Ching*

Plan to ponder:
Ask the prospective employer what he or she is trying to accomplish

Too often, job seekers focus on their own objectives, plans and backgrounds, rather than those of the person who must decide whether to extend a job offer. Corporate sales trainer Stephan Schiffman orders his students to work some variation on the "what-are-you-trying-to-get-accomplished" question into the very first meeting with a prospective customer and to take copious notes on the reply that follows. The question, when answered properly and accompanied by a healthy spell of old-fashioned listening, has led to big sales for Schiffman's students (of which the author is one). It can lead to a job offer for you.

This is also a question that good businesspeople enjoy answering in detail. More often than not, they focus on the obstacles that are preventing them from attaining their most important objectives. That's good for you, because one of the surest ways to get an opportunity is to volunteer to take on a tough assignment that no one else feels like handling! By asking your interviewer exactly what he or she is hoping to get done, and then isolating the problem areas where you may be able to provide assistance in that regard, you'll be in a great position to establish a solid professional alliance that benefits both parties.

Plan to ponder:
Get a stopgap job

Near your actual target company's headquarters, get a stopgap job. Then stop in regularly in person to ask about the possibility of a job opening at the target company. During a recent radio interview, I spoke with a woman who wanted to get a job as a reporter at a particular newspaper. After being told that there were no openings, she found a stopgap job at a nearby company and then returned to the offices of the newspaper *every* single day, in person, to ask whether someone had died, gotten pregnant or resigned over the past 24 hours. After only a few days, the management of the paper concluded they were dealing with someone who had the makings of a pretty good reporter and offered her a job.

This extremely direct approach will not be greeted with enthusiasm by all prospective employers, but it is certainly one example of how one can sometimes use straight-ahead *chutzpah* to get the right job offer in a hurry.

Plan to ponder:
Ask for a temporary assignment

There are times when a temporary assignment is the best way of getting your foot in the door at a company where you know you could make a meaningful contribution.

Temporary work has the added benefit of supplying you with cold, hard cash while you're searching for the perfect full-time gig, which certainly counts for something. You may opt for an assignment through a temporary agency—many job seekers have turned these short-term jobs into full-time ones—but there's also something to be said for directly approaching a particular employer, one you've researched extensively, to ask about temporary work.

෨ ෨ ෨ ෨ ෨

Those, then, are some techniques to bear in mind when you must secure a job assignment in less than 10 days. As you apply them, please remember that a single no is *not* a judgment on your merits as a person—but a signal that there's not a match at *that employer* at *that time*. Keep at it!

Chapter 5

Techniques to help you get a job within 11 to 15 days

Perhaps you've just given or received your two-week notice. While it may seem like an eternity to sit at a desk you know you're destined to vacate, the time will go by fast. And if you don't have something lined up, you'll quickly learn that your savings will go fast, too.

If you are obligated to fulfill your two-week commitment to the company, try to take as many vacation or personal days as possible in order to get a jump on your job search. Or change your hours so that you can spend prime business time making contacts, scheduling interviews and otherwise tracking down gainful employment.

Make every effort to contact five to 10 presidents of target organizations every day. Schedule meetings during lunch hours, early in the morning or after hours when possible—take work time off if necessary.

Do your best, however, not to burn any bridges with your soon-to-be former employer. While you certainly must look out for your own interests, it's important to leave on as positive terms as possible.

If, on the other hand, you are freed of previous work commitments and have the next 11 to 15 days free to pursue a job, continue the strategies laid out in previous chapter: Contact as many company presidents as possible, schedule as many meetings as possible and consider the following strategies to land that job.

The barriers are not yet erected which can say to aspiring genius: "Thus far and no further."
—Ludwig van Beethoven

Plan to ponder: Target businesses experiencing seasonal rushes

In other words, review the business pages of your local newspaper for the last few weeks and find out which of the companies in your area are so busy they don't know what to do to meet customer demand. There are always companies in this category, no matter what time of year it is. These organizations are often looking for help *right now.*

Make a list of the companies that may be in this category in your area and don't exclude any organizations in unfamiliar industries. (You're looking for matches in particular skill areas, not necessarily matches in particular job titles.) Contact the companies directly—the higher you call in the organization, the better—and share one of your success stories, as outlined in Chapter 1.

Plan to ponder:
Call at a truly ungodly hour

Guess what? If you call lots and lots of prospective employers really early—say, 6:30 to 8:30 a.m.—a certain percentage of the top people at those organizations will be sitting at their desks trying to get a little work done before the rush starts. Sure, you'll be interrupting them by calling them at this hour, but you'll also be impressing them with your initiative. You'll also be convincing them that you're as much of a workaholic as they are, which won't hurt your chances.

This is a good compromise to consider if you cannot, for whatever reason, mount an aggressive telemarketing campaign along the lines discussed in Chapters 3 and 4. You may get more accomplished in the limited time available. See the advice in Chapter 1 on conducting your top-level telemarketing campaign, as well as the advice in Chapter 3 on managing your contacts with company voice-mail machines.

Plan to ponder:
Be a guest at a professional meeting

Target your networking contacts who are members of professional organizations or industry associations—even service organizations such as the Lions Club—and ask them to invite you to one of their meetings. Typically, the formal meeting part of these weekly or monthly get-togethers offers an opportunity for you, the guest, to be introduced to the attendees. This is a chance for you to stand up, smile, briefly identify yourself and mention that you're "currently seeking new career opportunities."

In addition, the meetings usually offer some time for socializing, small talk and business card-swapping. These meetings offer some wonderful synergy. Not only do you have your buddy working for you, perhaps pointing out those members who are business owners, executives or otherwise in a position to hire, the fact that you're a friend of a member—someone the others know and trust—means you walk in with a valuable endorsement.

Make the most of the contacts you make at such events. Now when you call their offices to set up a meeting, you've got an easier task. Because they already have met you, your job of selling yourself is now that much easier.

Luck is the residue of design.
—Branch Rickey

Plan to ponder:
If you're still working, make the most of resources still available to you

Many large companies, in the wake of downsizings, have instituted outplacement services for their employees. Certainly it couldn't hurt to tap into these resources, but the process tends to work slowly and is not guaranteed.

But beyond outplacement, there are other job-search avenues you should continue to explore—within your own company. First, check with the resources people to find out if there may be growth in other departments of the company or a place where your unique skills might be put to use.

But don't stop with the HR people: Take your contacts, in other departments (the higher up, the better) to lunch—find out the scoop, see if there are some opportunities for you beyond the obvious. You're a displaced writer? Perhaps the accounting department is struggling with its policies manual—a project that may take months to complete.

And, by all means, don't overlook talking to other employees who've been displaced. While it's true that people in such circumstances are often paranoid, territorial and looking out for their own security, you'll find just as many are willing to share leads and contacts with you as they progress with their own job search. Perhaps one of your soon-to-be former co-workers has discovered a new business that requires not one of you, but two!

Destiny is not a matter of chance. It is a matter of choice. It is not a thing to be waited for. It is a thing to be achieved.
—William Jennings Bryan

Plan to ponder: Track down you old boss

Even if you've been downsized (or fired, for that matter), appeals to former employers can often lead to job offers. More than one victim of a "restructuring" campaign has found that a call to a previous employer can result in an immediate assignment.

Does it surprise you to learn that managers at companies that decide to shed a quarter to a third of their work force often find themselves looking at a pretty chaotic office environment in the months immediately following? I don't think so. Call your former employer and ask if there's anything you can help out with. In quite a few cases, job seekers have found that the answer is an instant yes. (You should be prepared to accept short-term contract work at first in such a situation, but bear in mind that this type of assignment may well serve as a stepping-stone for reentry on a full-time basis.)

One of the advantages of keeping your address book up-to-date is that doing so allows you to keep track of supervisors who have moved on to other organizations. If you know of anyone who falls into this category, you should certainly give the person a call and explain that you're looking for an opportunity to make a contribution on a professional level.

A man of genius makes no mistakes. His errors are volitional and are the portals of discovery.
—James Joyce

ભ ભ ભ ભ ભ

Can you find not just a job, but the right job, within 11-15 days? Sure you can. But remember that the key to doing so is in seeing opportunity in exactly the spot where others might see obstruction.

Chapter 6

Techniques to help you get a job within 16 to 20 days

The more time you have to land that job, the less motivated you might be to invest the effort, time and emotional energy required to do so. Let's face it: Job hunting is *not* the most fulfilling activity. It can be discouraging, demanding and a real lesson in humility.

But at this stage of the game, it's crucial to put as much effort into the job search as you would if you were pressed to find a job in a week. So set your alarm for 6 a.m., put on your business uniform and put in a minimum eight-hour day to make that new employment situation happen before 20 days is up.

Contact three to five presidents of target organizations every day, no matter what, and ask each to set up a meeting with you. See the advice in Chapter 2 for tips on strategizing your top-level telemarketing campaign.

Plan to ponder:
Bring a conversation piece

Bring a job search related conversation piece with you everywhere you go—and strike up conversations about it as often as possible. A conversation piece is exactly that: something you use to make guiding your way into an initial encounter with someone a little easier than it might otherwise be. If you are trying to track down the right job in a hurry, you can do worse than to find some object to wear, carry or produce at an opportune moment—an object that makes it easy for you to approach others and them to approach you.

People have gotten jobs by wearing T-shirts bearing abbreviated versions of their resume; by passing out fliers in the middle of busy train stations; and by handing out coffee and doughnuts to strangers.

You can take a direct approach, which those ideas represent—you'll probably see results fairly soon if you do—or you can select a more "passive" employment-related conversation piece. This might, to give just a few examples, be a camera (if you want to work as a photographer), a specially constructed badge or button (one that points the reader toward something related to the type of work you're after), or a large book on a topic related to the field of employment you're trying to enter.

Don't wait for people to approach you—begin an exchange by mentioning the conversation object yourself any time the opportunity presents itself in a social situation. Briefly share one of your success stories.

By the way, there's nothing wrong with completely neutral, nonjob-related conversation pieces, such as a sweatshirt bearing the name of a local sports team. Anything that helps you break the ice with strangers and point the conversation toward your job search is worth considering.

This technique works best when you have something you can pass along that helps the person you've been talking to contact you after the fact. I strongly recommend ace counselor Tony Dias's notion of putting a two- or three-sentence "resume" together on a business card, complete with contact information, and then passing these cards out to anyone and everyone you meet. Such cards work well as supplements to your conversation piece—or as conversation pieces themselves! Incorporate a trace of humor into the card (i.e., "A Small Resume for a Big Salesperson," if you're a little on the portly side), and you'll find that the initial contacts with people you don't know go a little better.

Don't waste time on the conversation-piece idea if taking the initiative for meeting and greeting new acquaintances, face to face and "out of the blue," is a painful experience for you. Find something else in the book. If you do select this approach, keep at it, and take down as many names and addresses as you can for follow-up purposes.

See, also, the advice in Chapter 3 on contacting everyone you know and telling them that you are looking for work in a particular area. Obviously, you won't need conversation pieces with these people—but the general philosophy behind the two ideas is essentially the same, and you could do worse than to put both into practice. *The more people you talk to, the faster you are likely to develop an employment lead that is right for you.*

You can't be afraid to make mistakes. You've got to play the game aggressively.

—Lou Piniella

Plan to ponder:
Follow the obituaries

Okay, it's a little morbid. But you're trying to find a way to help people solve problems, right? And what bigger problem is there than when someone who's more or less irreplaceable dies unexpectedly? Let's face it, it happens, and it may well be happening in a way that affects your job search. The newspaper will probably lay out what the person in question did for a living and where he or she worked. Look, no one said getting a job was going to consist entirely of things you can tell your mother about.

This gambit can be particularly effective if you follow a number of major city papers at once and you demonstrate, in a compelling way, your willingness to relocate to the target employer. Of course, if you spot a possible opening in your chosen field within your own geographical area of choice, so much the better.

Three points to bear in mind: Tact, tact and tact. The aim is to help people make sense of a strange new situation, not swoop down like a vulture. Express remorse for the person's passing and gingerly ask what the organization's plans are for the future in the area in question. The higher up you go in the organization, the likelier you are to get a straight answer—and meaningful job leads.

Be sensitive to the time. But don't be afraid to offer specific suggestions about how the organization might pick up the pieces and move on. Share the success stories you developed in Chapter 1, but don't make the mistake of bad-mouthing the last person who held the job!

The world is round. The place which may seem like the end may also be only the beginning.
—Ivy Baker Priest

Plan to ponder:
Send a series of mysterious faxes,
each with a power quote

This should be a quote that affects the decision-maker (ideally, the president of the organization), culled from a source he or she would not ordinarily review. The idea here is to cite a newspaper or trade magazine that regularly features articles that *affect* the prospective employer, but that is not directly *aimed* at the employer. (In a printing-industry magazine, for instance, you might spot an article about paper price increases that would be of interest to the head of a publishing company.)

Collect three or four such news items, spaced a day or so apart then fax them to the decision-maker and *do not mention employment.* Sign each fax message with your name, but do not supply return contact information. Then, after a week or so of this, contact the person directly, identify yourself and ask to get together for a meeting to discuss employment opportunities. This technique is best directed at presidents and CEOs.

Don't simply photocopy the article. Retype it in a legible and distinctive way. Keep the message to one page. Cite your source. Reproduce the quote verbatim.

Incorporate some consistent graphic element that ties the mystery faxes together. That way, when you call, you can say, "I've been sending along the bulletins with the small moose in the upper left-hand corner. I thought we could get together and talk about how I can help increase your sales revenues as a member of your sales staff."

What you send will shape what the decision-maker thinks of you. Keep your bulletins brief. Focus on issues of *direct importance* to the company: the introduction of new technologies, the actions of competitors, the consideration of legislation that will affect the company's business in a positive or negative way. Do not send frivolous or irrelevant materials!

If you use this technique, do so with multiple decision-makers; don't focus all your efforts on a single president.

Plan to ponder:
Sneak up on 'em while they're thinking about something else

Here's one way to make direct contact with the decision-makers in your field: Pay to attend a conference or seminar in your area of interest and then simply introduce yourself to everyone in sight.

Let's say your aim is to get a job in the insurance industry. Your objective would be to find some way to attend some seminar, training session or conference at which insurance executives are the primary audience—at an industry-wide gathering, for instance—and make full use of the time before, after and during the break periods of the main events. That's when you'll find the movers and shakers are probably in the mood to make or solidify contacts. Your objective would be to walk up to everyone, and I do mean everyone, introduce yourself, and say what it is you're hoping to contribute to your next employer. Using your business-card-sized resume (see page 93) is a good idea, as is vowing to make contact with every person in the room. Your persistence and good spirit in making contact will help you stand out. But remember—your "work time," the time for which you've paid good money, is the time between the main events! When everyone else is on break, you get to swing into action.

Plan to ponder:
Get to know a headhunter

It's not necessarily a lock that you'll get a job by enlisting the help of a qualified representative of the employment services industry, but you may decide that this method is worth a try. Good headhunters, the kind who can help you focus your objectives and sharpen up your resume, are an asset to your job search campaign; bad ones tend to consume more of your time than they deserve, and that makes you wonder about their real motives. If anyone tries to charge you for the privilege of "circulating" a resume to a "database" of employers, beware. There's a chance something fishy is going on. (Most reputable members of the industry are paid by the employer, not the prospective employee.)

Plan to ponder:
Use unusual information as a means
of initiating contact

No, we're not talking about blackmail. The idea is to track down some piece of useful information that most other job seekers would not appeal to, simply because they wouldn't know about it. This could take the form of searching for the e-mail address of someone who recently interviewed you, and then citing your persistence—and your superior online research technique—as a qualification for the job when you make contact via cyberspace. You must, of course, relate exactly how you tracked the information down. (There's a World Wide Web page available on the Internet know as "Who's Where" that allows one to identify the e-mail addresses of other people. The address is http://www.whowhere.com.)

Once again, let me remind you that you must be absolutely certain your recipient understands that your interest is of a *nonthreatening, professional* nature. In other words, make it clear that you're looking for a job—nothing more, nothing else.

If you bear this advice in mind, there are any number of potentially helpful variations to this "hyperpersonalized" approach that you can incorporate to generate quick results in your job search campaign. I heard about one job seeker who found out when a prospective employer was about to move and volunteered his services. I also learned about a person who volunteered to coach the soccer team of the children of the top decision-maker—in order to network with that decision-maker on the weekends. Both unorthodox techniques resulted in job offers. Using these opportunities to broadcast your success stories may well pay off. But beware of trying to "wear an employee down" by one of these methods!

ശ ശ ശ ശ ശ

Bear in mind that getting the job that's right for you—whether in 16 days or 16 weeks—is really a matter of developing and maintaining alliances through careful planning. It also requires confidence, optimism and enthusiasm.

Chapter 7

Techniques to help you get a job within 21 to 25 days

Delays have dangerous ends.
—William Shakespeare

Whether you're still employed but have just been given notice of the impending "reorganization" next month, or you're free to pursue job opportunities now, you must approach your job search with a commitment as if it were your full-time job.

If you're no longer employed, structure your weeks as if they were regular "9-to-5" days—and you're working overtime. Get up, get dressed, get on the phone or get in the car and seek out those prospective jobs each and every day of the week. If you're still committed to a job, do whatever you can to free up as much time as possible to pursue a job.

Set up a goal to contact company decision-makers, at least two a day if you're employed, more if you're not. Schedule immediate interviews and meetings.

Plan to ponder:
Set up a resume on a business card

Tell every single person you know that you are looking for work in a particular area. Yes, I do mean *everyone*. Your best bet here is probably to have a condensed, three-to-four-sentence version of your resume printed up on a business card, complete with your 24-hour contact information, and then to distribute these to your relatives, close friends, former employers, teachers and colleagues, and any attorneys, accountants, and/or consultants your relatives and close friends can refer you to. (Get names!)

The resume-on-a-business-card technique was first suggested to me by ace career counselor Tony Dias; a full treatment of this innovative technique appears in my book *303 Off-the-Wall Ways to Get a Job.* You can have the cards made up quite inexpensively—or even buy peel-and-stick magnetic attachments that will turn them into refrigerator magnets! One hint—don't go too heavy on the text. There's not room for a doctoral thesis, just a couple of sentences based on the success stories you developed.

Think this idea is a little far-fetched? Stop right now and take a look at your address book. You will probably find something on the order of 100 to 150 people you know on a first-name basis. If you stop and think for a moment, you can probably add another 50 to 75 names to the list. (If you need reference help, dust off that holiday-card list you update every December.) If you adopt this approach, every single one of the people you know *must* be advised of the fact that you're in the job market.

You should probably ask each for referrals of other people you can talk to. Remember, we live in an era where geography counts for very little. Even that friend of yours in New Zealand may be able to provide you with an important employment lead after you zap off an appropriate piece of e-mail outlining what you're looking for.

This method isn't *mandatory,* but I would certainly recommend it highly. If you decide to pursue this avenue, I recommend that you try to make at least 20 contacts with people in your circle of acquaintance *per day.* (Getting through to them should be a heck of a lot easier than getting through to the people at your target companies!)

Dreams are the touchstones of our characters.
—Henry David Thoreau

Plan to ponder:
Know your prospective employer

During your interview (or while trying to arrange an interview), recite, from memory, a portion of the company's annual report. You're applying for a position in order to help make a contribution to the organization. In order to do that, the prospective employer is convinced you will have to be trained and, to a certain degree, indoctrinated in the "culture" of the organization. One great (and easy!) way to elicit support from the decision-maker on this front is to quote, verbatim, important passages from annual reports, sales brochures or, even better, the CEO's own book if such a thing exists.

Whatever the "Bible" of the organization is, you can accelerate things if you find it, memorize several sizable chunks of it and recite these chunks at appropriate points during the interview. The interviewer will almost certainly conclude that you're the type of person who'll take the initiative when it comes to the training process. (And here I'm referring not just to the process of telling you about the specific tasks associated with your job, but to the intricate web of beliefs, alliances and behaviors that make up the target company's "corporate culture.) Reciting the "good book" convinces people that you are willing to make the effort to become one of the team. That helps—and speeds up—your cause.

Practice until you know your passage(s) cold. Use a tape recorder if necessary.

If, during your interview, you have not been presented with a question that provides you with a comfortable opportunity to recite the passages you have memorized, use the "do-you-have-any-questions-for-us" part of the interview, near the end of the meeting, to work the passage into the conversation. ("I'd just like to say that I'm very much looking forward to working for an organization that is, as your founder puts it...")

God helps them who help themselves.
—Benjamin Franklin

Plan to ponder:
Bring a visual display to the interview

Most interviewers are bored to tears by the task that faces them. And no wonder! They have essentially the same conversation with one applicant after another, and they sometimes spend hours on end staring at the same basic information, presented in almost unvarying formats. One way to ensure that you stand out from the pack with every interviewer—and thereby accelerate your progress toward the right job offer—is to incorporate *concise* visual representations of your success stories in the form of charts, drawings, graphs and the like.

Wait for the proper moment in the interview. After being presented with a question that bears directly on one of your success stories, say that you have brought along some materials that will help you answer the question and ask for permission to set them up. (This will be granted!) *Briefly* appeal to the information on your chart, photo, drawing or whatever. Then take a seat.

Obviously, neatness counts. Color captures attention! The whole idea behind this technique is to share some visual stimulation with people who are in desperate need of it. Use color to make your points in a compelling, dramatic way.

Stay away from violent or off-color imagery. It may capture the attention of your interviewers, but it won't win you any points for professionalism.

The highest part of the art of life is the expectation of miracles.
—William Bolitho

Plan to ponder:
Start at the bottom

Take a janitorial or other support position within the target company you want to work for—on the condition that a key decision-maker offer you ongoing "advice" in your field of choice within the target company. This is a time-honored maneuver that plays heavily on that age-old human motivator, guilt. Well, let's be honest, wanting to take full advantage of the talents of an underutilized employee plays a part, too. The idea is to show unflagging dedication to the duties associated with a job that isn't particularly difficult to get—and thereby audition for a job that is. Your specific interest in another type of work, and in working for the target company, should be stated outright. You should also consider specifying the timeline you're looking at.

There are potential drawbacks aplenty with this one; none of them are so severe as to merit removing the notion from consideration completely, but all of them are worth reviewing before you decide this idea is for you.

For one thing, you may well hook up with a supervisor who doesn't much care about your long-term career aspirations and who simply wants to get the halls swept this month. Do a little in-depth interviewing of your own before you commit.

For another thing, if you're working full- or part-time at this company, you significantly decrease the amount of time available to make contacts with decision-makers at others. The let-me-scrub-the-toilets approach is best reserved for a company you know is right for you, and one that you feel confident can benefit from your talents. Consider part-time work before full-time work. That way, you'll have part of the day left over to employ some of the other ideas in this book.

You write, "It is impossible." That is not French.
—Napoleon Bonaparte

Any lapse in morale or outlook will probably be fatal. Remember, you are putting your optimism on display in a lesser position in order to gain entry to a more important one. If you have any doubts about your ability to do this, you should not try this technique.

All the above problems having been duly outlined, it seems fair to point out, too, that some variation on this technique has been working wonders for job seekers for generations. Applied conscientiously and with a positive attitude, it may just deliver results for you.

Plan to ponder:
Use weird stationery and/or props to wake up your cover letter

This strategy is an interesting alternative to the "unusual resume" approach outlined in an earlier chapter. Here, the resume, though targeted, is pretty much standard-issue in appearance, but the cover letter is, shall we say, a little more creative.

During a recent series of radio interviews, I encountered job seekers who had used the following techniques and gotten a job in short order as a result: writing the cover letter on a burger wrapper from a fast-food outlet (complete with the legend "Don't let me be the next Burger Queen of the tri-state area"); attaching a two-headed quarter to a cover letter that reads, "Heads, you hire me, heads, you hire me"; and attaching a small pair of plastic sunglasses to the letter beneath the legend, "There's more to this candidate than meets the eye."

That's pretty creative stuff, and all of it is vouched for by the various job seekers as the kind of thing likely to make an employer snap to and take notice, at least for a moment.

Before you consider adapting any of these techniques, though, let me remind you that all of the advice concerning research and self-evaluation that you have read about in the earlier sections of this book still apply. What you know about and have to offer to the company in question must be an integral part of any "off-the-wall" job-search techniques you choose to apply. Get noticed, yes—but then follow through with success stories that display an appropriate level of knowledge about the challenges the employer is likely to face.

❧ ❧ ❧ ❧ ❧

Acting appropriately to develop new opportunities on the employment front (or in any other situation, for that matter), means recognizing that there is potential benefit in virtually any situation. The ancient Chinese oracle *The Book of Changes* writes, "It will be advantageous to be firm and correct, and thus there will be free course and success. Let the reader nourish a docility like that of a cow, and there will be good fortune." This advice is not an order to become completely passive in our dealings with people; instead it refers to acting in an inspired, discerning way that allows us to take advantage of complete harmony—and so-called "coincidence"—when we encounter others. If there is better advice to be passed along when it comes to making connections with the people who have it in their power to hire you, I certainly haven't come across it yet.

Chapter 8

Techniques to help you get a job within 26 to 30 days

Now that you've read through the preceding chapters—where we addressed the goals of landing a job in as little as one day to as many as 25 days, you probably feel that 26 to 30 days to find a job is a luxury. You can kick back, leisurely peruse the Sunday classifieds as you nurse your coffee, right? Spend some time polishing your resume, or maybe take a series of career exploration workshops.

Don't relax yet! Save that for your first vacation—after you land your job. Even though we have a little more breathing room here, it's still important to pursue your job search with the same intensity and commitment as if you had to land the job tomorrow. A month goes by a lot faster than you think.

Still, maintaining your positive attitude and rewarding yourself for your vigilant efforts remains an important part of the game plan here. So as you schedule your phone calls, information interviews and job canvassing, make sure to work in some time for pleasure as well.

As advised in previous chapters, you should plan to put in a full-time search effort, unless you're still employed. Get up every morning, the same time you did when you had a job to go to. Put on your business attire, check with your day planner and get started—whether it's making cold calls, follow-up appointments, going out for interviews, pursuing networking opportunities—or investigating one of the strategies in this chapter:

Contact at least one president of a target organization every day, no matter what, and ask him or her to set up a meeting with you for the next day. See the advice in Chapter 2 for tips on strategizing your top-level telemarketing campaign. Your library research should lead you toward contact information for at least 30 target companies (preferably smaller, entrepreneurial ones) before you try this. Review the ideas outlined in Chapters 2 through 7. The points you will find discussed in those chapters are meant for job search plans that have somewhat more aggressive deadlines. Review your job search plan and customize your approach for this "lengthier" time period for finding a job.

Plan to ponder:
Get a job to find a job

Pick a stopgap job that allows you some form of contact with people likely to be willing to network with you about employment opportunities—and then make the most of those opportunities. In other words, if you have to take on a job that doesn't really represent what motivational trainer Anthony Robbins calls your "magnificent obsession," pick one that might lead in that direction. Consider accepting a "B-level" job that allows you plenty of exposure to the public in general, and to potential decision-makers in your field of interest in particular. Then, discreetly and while maintaining all the duties of your "real" job, keep an eye open for chances to make your case to prospective employers.

I've heard about people who furthered their careers by talking themselves up during stints as parking lot attendants, chatting during telemarketing assignments and working in restaurants they knew to be frequented by decision-makers. The key is to be willing (and eager) to talk about your aspirations at literally any opportunity.

Be sure that the stopgap job you line up is one that has a realistic chance of putting you in front of the types of people you want to work for. (For instance, if you want to work in the financial industry, you might decide that a short-term job in a financial-district parking lot could give you enough exposure to key people to mount a business-card-sized-resume-on-the-dashboard campaign.) Perform all your official duties fully and conscientiously.

Keep it quiet when necessary. Supervisors are likely to frown on on-the-job career networking.

It is morale that wins the victory.
—George C. Marshall

I hit anything that's close to the plate. I don't wait for that one pitch.

—Rod Carew

Plan to ponder:
Make the customer connection

Sometimes companies are extremely eager to talk to people who have become intimately familiar with their product or service *as customers*. Is there an employment connection you can try to make in this area? If you have a strong sense of the target company's market, are good at repairing (or selling) the product or service in question and *know the company more or less inside and out,* you may stand a good chance in this area.

Most important, of course, is to have an abiding passion for the product or service. If you love a particular model of car, could you work as a salesperson for a dealership that represents it? If you are a whiz at a certain video game manufactured by a local firm, could you help contribute to its testing and quality control efforts in new product development? Call the top person in the organization as outlined in Chapter 2 and make your case.

Research is everything in this case—but, fortunately, you'll be researching something you already love, which is the very best kind of library work!

Remember, though, that you must present yourself not simply as a customer who wants to work for the firm, but as one who has taken the trouble to find out as much as humanly possible about the company in question.

Taking your application directly to the top is always a good idea, but it's particularly important here. CEOs and other bottom-line types may be the only ones capable of seeing the potential value of eliciting the aid of a savvy customer as an employee. The rest of the crew may keep asking how many years you've worked in the industry on a salaried basis, since that's what's on their checklist of interview questions.

Do the best you can and don't worry about the criticisms. Once you accept the fact that you're not perfect, then you develop some confidence.

—Rosalyn Carter

Plan to ponder:
Offer to work on a reduced-salary basis for the first 30 days

An unusual gambit to be sure, but one that can perhaps be incorporated into your top-level telemarketing campaign with success. This is a lower-voltage variation on the "make-an-iron-clad-guarantee" technique outlined in Chapter 3. It takes some of the risk out of the equation for the employer by reducing the up-front investment. Of course, it also reduces your up-front income...but in some cases, this approach may be a realistic one for entry into a new field.

Don't agree to any reduced-salary arrangement until you can establish exactly what the benchmarks will be for measuring satisfaction with your performance and exactly what the salary will be once you pass muster with the employer. (You will have accelerated the process somewhat and must be willing to deal with the specifics of salary negotiation fairly early on, if you try this.)

Plan to ponder:
A twist on the reduced salary strategy

This twist to the previous strategy may be more effective, particularly if you're selling the employer on a position for which there isn't an opening. Consider asking about part-time hours for a probationary period. If the employer is not yet ready to make a full-time commitment to you, you should feel comfortable reserving your own time for other income-producing or job-canvassing possibilities.

Plan to ponder:
Use a "teaser" mailing campaign

This is a technique that uses the mails to baffle the prospective employer over a period of time—and win interest that you can exploit during a follow-up call. If you wanted to win a job as a salesperson, for instance, you might send the decision-maker a (sharp-looking) color cartoon of a door slamming and nothing else. No address, no phone number, no text. Just a small picture of a door slamming, complete with sound effects. Once you've done this, you would follow up with a slightly larger picture of a door slamming. One the decision-maker would receive, say, two days after the first message. Then you would send a third image—the largest picture yet of a door slamming.

By this point, your decision-maker is likely to be wondering who on earth is sending the strange cartoons.

That's good. When you finally send your targeted cover letter and resume, both will lead off with a headline that reads, "If you're looking for someone who knows how to close a sale, look no further!" And both will feature reduced versions of the cartoon. When you call to follow up on your mailing, you won't be the person who had a resume that looks just like everyone else's—you'll be the one who sent the letters most likely to be remembered! (You should, of course, make reference to the image during your initial conversation with the decision-maker.)

We act as though comfort and luxury were the chief requirements of life, when all that we need to make us really happy is something to be enthusiastic about.

—Charles Kingsley

అ అ అ అ అ

There's nothing particularly enjoyable about the financial and social pressures associated with having to find a job in a hurry. But my hope, as we close this book, is that you've found something to focus on that's exciting and perhaps even a little inspiring, about the challenge of hooking up with the right potential employer.

By using the strategies outlined in this book, you're probably going to see the task of seeking employment in an entirely new way when you take the time to:

- Isolate your strong suits and impressive past accomplishments.
- Use creative ways to contact top decision-makers.
- Use your job search to demonstrate how you deal with potentially challenging situations.

You'll be doing a lot more than impressing the people who are considering hiring you. You'll be changing the way you look at yourself. Once you start looking at yourself not simply as an employee, but as a prospective business partner, and a pretty sharp one at that, things start falling into place. And believe me, looking at yourself as a business partner is a habit worth cultivating in today's occasionally unpredictable economy—because no matter how many *employees* a key decision-maker may think are necessary, he or she is always on the lookout for new *allies*. When you move beyond the "only-following-orders" stage, take responsibility for your own results and help others achieve their important goals, an ally is what you become.

Here's to mastering the two neglected arts of the employment world: making your own breaks and forging new partnerships as an equal. May you find the opportunity to enjoy them both!

Appendix 1

Sample forms

Sample contact log form

An example of a form you can adapt to your telephone contact work is on page 116. Don't try to keep information for 20 of your prospective employers on the same sheet of paper. Photocopy the form provided and you'll have enough room to take down all the information you need for each firm. Bind the sheets in a notebook.

Remember: The *quicker* you want to get a job, the *more* prospective employers you should be contacting. Getting lulled into a false sense of security by a single "nibble" is what causes many job searches to stall. Make as many copies of the form as you need—then hit the library (to identify the companies you will be calling) and then the telephones!

When in doubt, call the president and/or his or her assistant.

Last Minute Job Search Tips

Company Name:_____

Telephone:_____

Date of first call:_____

Contact:_____

Notes:_____

_____

Next step:_____

Second call:_____

Contact:_____

Notes:_____

_____

Next step:_____

Third call:_____

Contact:_____

Notes:_____

_____

Next step:_____

Fourth call:_____

Contact:_____

Notes:_____

_____

Next step:_____

Company's requirements for open position:

_____

_____

_____

Important: *Have you verified the spelling of the contact's name?*
Have you asked for a formal or informal job description for the job you want?
Has this company been sent a targeted resume and letter based on that job description?

Sample targeted resume

In the resume on page 118, notice how the applicant has pointed the "career objective" portion of his resume directly toward the position for which he is applying *at this company*. If you don't want to revise your objective in this way, you should probably skip it altogether.

There are other strong points to this resume. Notice how nearly every aspect of it points directly or indirectly to writing, journalism or copy development skills. (If the applicant were applying for a job that didn't highlight these skills, he'd have to find other parts of his background to emphasize!) The only part of the resume that doesn't focus in some way on writing skills is the final paragraph about volunteer work, which highlights a significant, quan-tifiable increase in membership for which the applicant was responsible. Talk about bottom-line awareness!

AARON BENJAMIN
4175 Central Avenue
Brambleton, IL 60999
(312) 555-6775

Job Objective: Writer in Corporate Publications Department.

Education: Bachelor of Arts, Indiana University, 1994
Major: Journalism/Minor: Government
GPA: 3.5/4.0

Related
Experience: *Indiana Daily Student* (student newspaper):
Features Editor, 1995-1996
Editorial Page Editor, 1994-1995
Staff Reporter, 1993-1994

Work
Experience: *Brambleton Weekly Times:* Reporter, Business
Department, summers, 1991-1993
Wrote features on business owners and other
business-related news in Brambleton area;
edited copy of other writers. Trained new
interns in business department.

Honors/
Awards: Ernie Pyle Scholarship, Journalism Department,
1991 finalist, Sigma Delta Chi writing awards,
1992.

Community
Activities: **Member, Steering committee, Cancer**
Awareness Campaign
Responsible for disseminating information
(writing ad copy, public speaking) on health
issues to campus audiences.

Vice President, Big Brothers campus
chapter
Founded and developed first membership
drive for college Big Brother program;
increased chapter membership by 150% in
3 months.

Sample targeted cover letter

Here's a nice example of a targeted cover letter that gets right to the point.

Alan Bell
463 Hammerton Way
Cambridge, MA 02138

May 25, 1996

Ms. Ellen Sharp, Director of Sales
Betterway Optical Equipment
656 Gerard Street
Boston, MA 02254

Dear Ms. Sharp:

After a brief discussion today with Becky, your receptionist, I think I've identified some of the most important factors you're looking for in a new sales manager:

- The ability to react quickly to sudden market shifts. (I guided the most successful launch of a new product in my company's history, the Presto-Scanner, and identified new corporate markets that accounted for 40,000 unit sales.)

- Strong familiarity with the optical industry. (I have attended the last four Optic World industry conferences as a representative of my current firm, and have followed your company's growth with great interest by keeping up with *Optics Journal.*)

- Ability to deliver bottom-line results. (Sales revenue in the department I currently manage has increased by at least 20% in each of the past four years.)

I'd like to talk to you about making a contribution to your firm as a full-time employee. Enclosed please find my resume. I'll call you at 9:30 a.m. on Wednesday, April 3, to make sure these materials reached you.

Sincerely,

Alan Bell

Alan Bell

P.S.: If we can get together for an interview to discuss the current opening, I guarantee that you will be glad you did so.

Appendix 2

For further reference

Career Press editors, *Resumes! Resumes! Resumes!*, Career Press, Franklin Lakes, NJ, 1995.

Fry, Ron, *101 Great Answers to the Toughest Interview Questions, 3rd ed.*, Career Press, Franklin Lakes, NJ, 1996.

Fry, Ron, *Your First Interview, 3rd ed.*, Career Press, Franklin Lakes, NJ, 1996.

Fry, Ron, *Your First Job, 2nd ed.*, Career Press, Franklin Lakes, NJ, 1996.

Fry, Ron, *Your First Resume, 4th ed.*, Career Press, Franklin Lakes, NJ, 1996.

King, Julie Adair, *The Smart Woman's Guide to Interviewing and Salary Negotiation, 2nd ed.*, Career Press, Franklin Lakes, NJ, 1993.

Schiffman, Stephan, *Asking Questions, Winning Sales,* Workshops on Tape, New York, NY, 1996.

Toropov, Brandon, *303 Off-the-Wall Ways to Get a Job,* Career Press, Franklin Lakes, NJ, 1995.

About the author

Brandon Toropov is a Boston-area writer who served as editor for a number of job-search bestsellers. His works include *303 Off-the-Wall Ways to Get a Job* and the companion volume to this book, *Last Minute Interview Tips*.

His other books include the forthcoming *Who Was Eleanor Rigby?*, a book of Beatles trivia questions, and *The Everything Christmas Book*, on which he served as general editor.

Index